I0799077

rockin'
around
rockin'
around

Rockin' around the Christmas Tree
A FESTIVE GUIDE TO CELEBRATING THE HOLIDAYS
Recipes, Crafts, and More!
HO HO
HARPER Celebrate

Rockin' Around the Christmas Tree
Copyright © 2025 HarperCollins Focus LLC

Published under permission/license from St. Nicholas Music Inc. *Rockin' Around the Christmas Tree* © 1958 (Renewed 1986) St. Nicholas Music Inc., All Rights Reserved. Any duplication, adaptation, arranging, and/or transmission of this copyrighted musicrequires the written consent of the copyright owner(s) and of St. Nicholas Music. Unauthorized uses are infringements of the copyright laws of the United States and other countries and may subject the user to civil and/or criminal penalties.

ROCKIN' AROUND THE CHRISTMAS TREE is a trademark of St. Nicholas Music Inc. and is registered in the United States. All rights reserved.

All rights reserved. No portion of this book may be reproduced, stored in a retrieval system, or transmitted in any form or by any means—electronic, mechanical, photocopy, recording, scanning, or other—except for brief quotations in critical reviews or articles, without the prior written permission of the publisher.

Published by Harper Celebrate, an imprint of HarperCollins Focus LLC.

Any internet addresses (websites, blogs, etc.) in this book are offered as a resource. They are not intended in any way to be or imply an endorsement by HarperCollins Focus LLC, nor does HarperCollins Focus LLC vouch for the content of these sites for the life of this book.

ART DIRECTION by Jen Showalter Greenwalt
EDITORIAL DIRECTION by Kara Mannix
COVER AND INTERIOR ILLUSTRATIONS by Lulu Dubreuil
INTERIOR DESIGN by Kathy Mitchell
PHOTO CREDITS © Lines+Angles

ISBN 978-1-4002-5258-9 (Audiobook)
ISBN 978-1-4002-5254-1 (epub)
ISBN 978-1-4002-5256-5 (HC)

Printed in Vietnam

25 26 27 28 29 SEV 5 4 3 2 1

A TIMELESS SONG FOR THE SEASON

1 ✳ Rockin' around the Christmas tree FINDING THE PERFECT TREE 10

2 ✳ At the Christmas party hop HOSTING CHRISTMAS PARTIES 24

3 ✳ Mistletoe hung where you can see DECORATING WITH MISTLETOE 36

4 ✳ Every couple tries to stop CELEBRATING LOVE AT CHRISTMAS 46

5 ✳ Rockin' around the Christmas tree AN ODE TO ORNAMENTS 56

6 ✳ Let the Christmas spirit ring GETTING INTO THE CHRISTMAS SPIRIT 68

7 ✳ Later we'll have some pumpkin pie YUMMY CHRISTMAS SWEETS 80

8 ✳ And we'll do some caroling SINGING THROUGH THE SEASON 92

9 ✳ You will get a sentimental feeling REMEMBERING CHRISTMASES OF OLD 100

10 ✳ When you hear voices singing, "let's be jolly" BRINGING JOY TO THE WORLD . . 112

11 ✳ Deck the halls with boughs of holly HOME DECOR & GREENERY 122

12 ✳ Rockin' around the Christmas tree HAPPY CHRISTMAS MORNING! 132

13 ✳ Have a happy holiday COZY CHRISTMAS GATHERINGS 142

14 ✳ Everyone dancin' merrily HOLIDAY DANCE PARTY 152

15 ✳ In the new old-fashioned way MIXING CHRISTMAS PAST & PRESENT 164

A Timeless Song for the Season

Under the flickering lights of the department store, as your eyes search the shelves for your last-minute gift, you hear it. Or maybe you're on the floor, legs splayed, with scissors and tape and wrapping paper strewn nearby when your Spotify playlist puts it at the top of your queue. Perhaps you're watching Kevin McCallister throw a one-person Christmas dance party in *Home Alone* when that familiar song from your childhood pipes through your speakers.

Without any effort, you know all the words by heart. You can't help but sing them out loud or hum along while bopping to the catchy beat.

Rockin' around the Christmas tree
at the Christmas party hop.
Mistletoe hung where you can see,
every couple tries to stop.

Rockin' around the Christmas tree
let the Christmas spirit ring!
Later we'll have some pumpkin pie
and we'll do some caroling.

You will get a sentimental feeling
when you hear voices singing, "let's be jolly!"
Deck the halls with boughs of holly!

Rockin' around the Christmas tree
have a happy holiday.
Everyone dancin' merrily
in the new old-fashioned way!

Brenda Lee's 1958 rendition of "Rockin' Around the Christmas Tree" has traveled through time on the grooves of a vinyl record to our wireless earbuds today. And when you finally hear it for the first time during the holiday season, you know that Christmas has truly arrived.

A History of "Rockin'"

In 1957 "Little Brenda Lee" scored her first *Billboard* hit (at age twelve!). She would be named "the female artist of the decade" in the 1960s and would become the first "queen of rock 'n' roll." She was friends with Elvis and the Beatles, and John Lennon said that her voice "defines rock 'n' roll." With more than 100 million records sold, Brenda is one of the most successful recording artists in history.

But in July of 1958, Brenda stepped into a music studio in Nashville, where a Christmas tree stood and holiday decorations decked the halls. The thirteen-year-old singer lent her powerful voice, colored by the country-blues and gospel music of her roots, to a brand-new song penned by Johnny Marks, a songwriter from New York who had earned acclaim for writing "Rudolph the Red-Nosed Reindeer" and "A Holly Jolly Christmas."

The song was released that November but didn't chart on *Billboard* until two years later, when it peaked at #14. Though the song didn't receive massive public acclaim, the 45s spun throughout the season on record players around the country. Slowly "Rockin'"

became part of the holiday canon, and now it remains a nostalgic nod to the songs that came out of the prolific twenty-five-year period when pop music ushered Christmas songs into our hearts forever.

In 1990 Brenda, then in her mid-forties, received an unexpected phone call from a friend. "Have you seen the new movie *Home Alone*?" they asked. She hadn't. "Your song's all over it," they said and hung up.

"I thought, *Huh. What song are they talking about?* So I called them back and they said, 'Rockin' Around the Christmas Tree,' it's all over it! And that's when [the song] really got a big surge," the artist remembers.

Millennials were falling in love with the then-thirty-two-year-old song as they laughed at Kevin McCallister's antics to drive away the would-be burglars plotting to get into his family's home. The song was still in the hearts of generations old and new when, in 2014, another unexpected event happened: The song hit the *Billboard* chart for the first time since 1962, thanks to the new streaming era of music. *Billboard* counted all the plays the song was getting on YouTube and streamers like Spotify. And like clockwork, whenever the holiday season rolled around, "Rockin'" would reappear on the *Billboard* Hot 100, climbing a little more every year. In 2019 the song peaked at an astonishing #2, sixty-one years after its release. The next few years, the song stayed at its #2 peak, with the same song ahead of it every single time—Mariah Carey's "All I Want for Christmas Is You."

In 2023 Universal Music Group (UMG) released a music video for "Rockin'" featuring Brenda, her family, and two of her best friends: country music superstars Trisha Yearwood and Tanya Tucker. Viewers went wild for the video, sharing and resharing on social media, sending the video into viral territory.

Brenda's phone rang again that Christmas season. Sixty-five years after its release, for the first time in the song's history, "Rockin'" had hit #1 on the *Billboard* Hot 100.

And to mark the significant moment, Brenda, one of the first queens of rock 'n' roll, received a bouquet of flowers from the Queen of Christmas herself, Mariah Carey.

Why are we still so attached to this song more than six decades later? Perhaps because it touches on so many elements that make the holidays feel special: Christmas trees, decorating our homes, sweet treats, great music, remembering Christmases of old. It reminds us of the magic of the season and the people we share it with, and it gives us a chance to celebrate another year of life and love.

So let's keep the magic going!

Let the timeless lyrics of "Rockin' Around the Christmas Tree" be your guide for the holidays. In these pages, you'll find tons of ideas for celebrating the season in a new old-fashioned way." Whether you're looking for a killer cocktail to serve at your party, deciding which Christmas tree is right for your home, looking for ideas for stocking stuffers, or making your own DIY mistletoe wreath, we've got what you need.

Take inspiration from this timeless song, its sentimental lyrics and toe-tapping melody, and the spirit of Christmas it conveys as you decorate, dance, bake, celebrate—and, of course, *rock*—around your Christmas tree.

Rockin' around
the Christmas tree

Finding *the* PERFECT TREE

Magical Moments Start with the Tree

When does the Christmas season *really* begin? Is it when you hear the first Christmas song on the radio? Spy the first decoration as you're out and about? Or does Christmas begin on a certain day, like November 1 or the day after Thanksgiving? No matter what your marker is, one thing's for certain: When your tree goes up, the holiday season has officially begun.

It's easy to enjoy a Christmas tree—the piney scent of a fresh evergreen, the lights and decorations—they work together to remind us of the joy of past holidays and the thrill of memories yet to be made.

But when did these trees become linked with Christmas? For ancient cultures around the world, plants and trees that remained green through the winter held a special meaning. Many people hung boughs of fir, spruce,

Fun Fact!

President Franklin Pierce brought the first Christmas tree to the White House in the 1850s, but it was President Calvin Coolidge who, in 1923, began the tradition of the National Christmas Tree Lighting Ceremony. It is now held every year on the White House lawn.

and pine over their doors and windows, heralding life and the hope of spring to come.

Historical records from the 1500s indicate that Germans were the first to bring trees into their homes as a symbol for the sacred Christmas holiday. Some believe that Protestant reformer Martin Luther was walking home on a crisp winter night when he spied an evergreen sparkling in the snow among the twinkling stars and was moved by the sight. He brought the tree home and added lighted candles to the branches to recapture the scene for his family.

German settlers brought the Christmas tree to American homes in the 1800s. The tradition spread across the country, and as popularity for the trees grew, so did their size. Instead of the tabletop-sized trees originally used by Germans, Americans preferred trees that stretched from floor to ceiling. They decorated these trees mostly with edible ornaments like popcorn garlands, apples, nuts, and marzipan, though the trendiest decorators began using glass ornaments from Germany in the 1890s. The advent of electricity helped trees glow all night long and ushered Christmas trees out of homes and into town squares, making them a collective joy for the entire community.

Today, no matter where in the world the holiday takes you, the enduring symbol of the Christmas tree is sure to be nearby, beckoning you to spend some time celebrating beneath its branches.

CHOOSING YOUR TREE

A Christmas tree farm or market might look like a sea of evergreen. How do you pick a live tree that's right for you? What matters most: appearance? fragrance? ease of maintenance?

Here's a quick breakdown to help you decide:

TREE	APPEARANCE
Fraser Fir	Dark green needles with a silvery underside and strong branches, perfect for holding heavy ornaments
Blue Spruce	Blue-gray needles and a symmetrical shape, with a more formal appearance
Douglas Fir	Shiny blue-green needles that radiate in all directions from the branch
Balsam Fir	Dark green needles with a narrow, pyramidal shape
Scotch Pine	Bright green needles with stiff branches known for its full, dense shape
Silver Tip	Widely spaced branches and silver-tipped needles; a minimal, vintage look
Virginia Pine	Dense, dark green foliage with short, twisted needles that give it a bushy appearance

Fun Fact!

Christmas trees take about six to eight years to mature.

FRAGRANCE	NEEDLES
Mild and fresh	One of the best for lasting throughout the season
Mild and fresh	Can be sharp, making it less ideal for homes with young children or pets
Strong and sweet	May shed if not watered properly
Strong, classic scent	Good retention, with proper care
Mild and fresh	Excellent retention, even when dry
Mild and fresh	Good retention, with proper care
Moderately strong	Good retention, with proper care

Christmas Crunch

PREP TIME: 10 MINUTES / TOTAL TIME: 45 MINUTES / SERVES: 6 TO 8

Keep a bowl of this sweet-and-salty snack mix handy as you decorate the tree.

2 bags microwavable popcorn or ½ cup kernels, popped

1½ cups broken pretzel pieces

1 cup red M&M's

1 cup semisweet chocolate chips

▶ DIRECTIONS

1. In a large mixing bowl, combine the popcorn, pretzels, and M&M's. Transfer the mixture onto a sheet of waxed paper in a single layer.
2. Add the chocolate chips to a microwave-safe bowl and melt on 50 percent power in 15-to-30-second intervals, stirring after each interval until melted and smooth.
3. Dip the back of a spoon or a fork into the melted chocolate and drizzle evenly across the popcorn mixture. Let the chocolate cool.
4. Separate the mix into pieces and enjoy.

Try This: Make a double batch of the popcorn to use in a DIY Christmas tree garland (page 20).

Pro Tip: If you can't find just red M&M's, use the seasonal red and green mix or pick out the colors of your choosing.

Pro Tip: For an extra fun garnish, add shortbread cookies to your drinks or serve alongside.

Eggnog Cocktail

TOTAL TIME: 5 MINUTES / SERVES: 2

Make your tree decorating even more festive by dressing up this classic Christmas drink. Rich and creamy, eggnog is delicious with or without a shot of your favorite holiday spirit. You can use store bought or homemade eggnog in this recipe.

2 ounces dark rum

2 ounces brandy

1 cup eggnog

1/8 teaspoon nutmeg

1/8 teaspoon cinnamon

1/8 teaspoon ground star anise

1/2 teaspoon demerara or turbinado sugar

2 sticks cinnamon for garnish

2 pods star anise for garnish

DIRECTIONS

1. Mix the rum, brandy, and eggnog in a large cocktail shaker with ice.
2. Add the nutmeg, cinnamon, ground star anise, and sugar to a small plate. Wet the rim of a glass with rum. Roll the rim of the glass in the spices.
3. Strain the eggnog mixture between two glasses. Garnish with the cinnamon sticks and star anise pods, if desired.

MOCKTAIL MOMENT: *Instead of the liqueurs, add 1/4 cup water, 1 teaspoon espresso powder, and 1 tablespoon brown sugar to a saucepan. Stir together until it starts to boil, then remove the mixture from the heat. Cool before adding to the eggnog.*

Popcorn and Cranberry Garland

TOTAL TIME: 2 TO 3 HOURS / MAKES: 12 FEET OF GARLAND

Bring some nostalgic whimsy to your tree with this popcorn-and-dried-cranberry garland. (An added bonus: You can munch on your materials as you make it.)

1 spool white thread (or floral wire, fishing line, or dental floss)

1 sewing needle

12 cups plain popcorn, popped

6 cups dried cranberries or craisins

▶ INSTRUCTIONS

1. Thread the needle with your desired length of thread and make a large knot approximately 6 inches from the end.

2. Carefully slide the needle through the popcorn and cranberries alternately, using the desired pattern of your choice. When the garland is done, cut the needle off and create a large knot at the other end.

3. Wrap the garland around the tree or hang wherever you like.

Branch Out Beyond Tradition

Trees adorned with rich reds and greens are classic, but sometimes it's fun to shake things up. There are all kinds of trees with modern looks just waiting to deck your halls.

DIFFERENT TREE COLORS

Craving a new color palette for your holiday? There are all kinds of tree colors to match your decor, whether you like things pretty in pink or you're into calming neutrals.

DIFFERENT TREE STYLES

Your Christmas tree should fit *your* style. Whether your vibe is rustic farmhouse or city posh, minimalist or full-on formal decor, you can easily curate your tree to match your taste.

DIFFERENT TREE MATERIALS

You don't need an evergreen. Live by the beach? Use a palm tree. Enjoy the desert? Decorate a cactus. Love a vintage vibe? Break out the ceramic trees. Or even just spray paint some twigs for a minimal festive look.

At the Christmas party hop

Hosting CHRISTMAS Parties

A Time to Be with Others

What makes holiday gatherings feel so special? Is it the music that drifts from our speakers only a few weeks out of the year? Is it the boxes filled with Christmas cookies or the special Christmas dinner that's plated on the good china? Perhaps it's the decorations that adorn our walls and tabletops or the twinkling lights that line the rooftops as we walk in the crisp night air, the crunch of snow under our feet and the stars sparkling in the sky above. Maybe all these things add up to make the season feel magical.

But what would the holidays be if we didn't have other people to celebrate with?

Think back to your happiest holiday memories, and you're sure to see the faces that brought you joy. Christmas is made more special by the people we spend it with. Sometimes our holiday is full of the people we regularly spend our days with, and sometimes it brings people we haven't seen in a while back into our lives. We *ooh* over little ones who aren't so little anymore and *ahh* at the accomplishments of a talented friend. We see lines on faces we have known all our lives, familiar smiles that still bring warmth to our days.

Hosting a Christmas party is a surefire way to bring people together—old friends and new—and spread cheer in a simple way.

Fun Fact!

What is a "Christmas party hop"? In the 1950s, teens would take off their shoes and dance in their socks—in what was called a "sock hop"—to protect the gymnasium floor. Try going shoeless at your "party hop."

Sometimes we may feel that to celebrate the holidays "the right way" or make them memorable, our gathering should be over-the-top. But the holidays are special not because of how we celebrate but who we celebrate them with. In this section, you'll find tips and tricks to make hosting a gathering with your people feel fun, festive, and easy.

Spinach Artichoke Christmas Tree Snack

PREP TIME: 10 MINUTES / TOTAL TIME: 30 MINUTES / MAKES: 23 PIECES

Whether you're hosting a dinner party or a casual gathering, having a plate of savory nibbles will make it easy for your guests to snack while they chat.

2 ounces sliced prosciutto

1 cup artichoke hearts, drained and finely chopped

1/4 cup frozen chopped spinach, thawed and drained

1/2 cup grated Parmesan cheese

1/4 cup mayonnaise

1/4 cup sour cream

1/4 teaspoon kosher salt

1/4 teaspoon black pepper

1 long French baguette, cut into 23 thick rounds

1 sprig fresh thyme, chopped, for garnish

▶ DIRECTIONS

1. Preheat oven to 400 degrees F. Line a cookie sheet with parchment paper.

2. Lay each slice of the prosciutto on the prepared cookie sheet. Bake for about 10 minutes or until they begin to look crispy and have a deep red color.

3. Remove the crispy prosciutto from the oven. Let cool before breaking into small pieces.

4. Stir together the artichokes, spinach, Parmesan cheese, mayonnaise, sour cream, salt, and pepper in a large bowl.

5. Spoon about a tablespoon of the artichoke mixture on top of each slice of bread and place them on the cookie sheet used for the prosciutto. Bake for

about 10 minutes or until bread edges are slightly golden and topping is just starting to brown.

6. Remove from the oven and arrange into a tree pattern to serve. Garnish each toast with a piece of crispy prosciutto and sprinkle with fresh chopped thyme.

HOLIDAY TABLESCAPE

To prep for guests coming over, create a beautiful tablescape with what you already have.

STEP 1: START WITH THE FOUNDATION

- Decide on a tablecloth or let your table surface be the backdrop.
- Add a cloth runner to create visual interest and a central spot for your accessories to gather. A plank or a wooden cheese board can create a rustic vibe and also vary the height of the decor.

STEP 2: ADD ACCESSORIES

- Pinecones, holly leaves and berries, and evergreen stems bring the beauty of nature to your table.
- Use small or unique serving dishes to help special foods stand out.
- Taper candles lend a sleek look, while electric votives bring a soft lighting that'll last all night.
- Sprinkle in silk florals, ribbons, bows, and baubles to round out the scene.

STEP 3: ARRANGE PLACE SETTINGS

- Layer place settings with various dishes on top.
- Decide which placemats work best for your table. Neutral placemats can look great.
- For a special touch, wrap cloth napkins with twine. You can tuck in a sprig of holly or evergreen to add a pop of color.

Set Up a Self-serve Drink Station

As the party host, you already wear a lot of hats: chef, networker, DJ, emcee, wrangler of coats. So do yourself a favor: Take off the "bartender" hat and hand it to your guests. A self-serve drink station frees you up to enjoy the party a bit more while guests take care of their own beverage needs. A few pointers to keep in mind as you set up your station:

Choose drinks that are easy to make in bulk and can sit in a punch bowl or carafe for a while and still be delicious.

Hot adult beverages: a slow cooker or carafe of mulled wine or spiked cider with rum.

Cold cocktails: a pitcher of punch (the Cranberry Sleigh Ride, page 77, would work great for this).

Spirit-free: Make sure to include a drink that's alcohol-free for guests who don't wish to imbibe, like a hot cocoa or an iced coffee.

Make sure to put out plenty of cups and glasses.

Add some garnish options so guests can dress up their drinks. Candy canes, sugared cranberries, marshmallows, or sprinkles work well.

Drink charms can prevent guests from getting their drinks mixed up, and they can also act as festive decor.

Santa's Favorite Rum Cocktail

TOTAL TIME: 5 MINUTES / SERVES: 1

Rum isn't just for warm weather—that's what Santa thinks, anyway! Dark rum mixed with ginger ale and cinnamon brings a spicy warmth to this cocktail. It will be sure to delight Santa and your party guests too.

2 ounces dark rum

1 ounce herbal liqueur, such as Chartreuse

4 ounces ginger ale

Dried lemon wheel for garnish

Cinnamon stick for garnish

▶ DIRECTIONS

1. Add the rum and herbal liqueur to a glass filled with crushed ice. Top with the ginger ale and stir to combine.
2. Garnish with a dried lemon wheel and cinnamon stick.

PLANNING A CHRISTMAS PARTY? REMEMBER THESE DOS AND DON'TS!

DO: SEND INVITES EARLY.

Schedules tend to fill up this time of year. When the calendar turns from October to November, it's time to choose a date for the party and get those invites out.

DON'T: GUILT PEOPLE INTO COMING.

People have so many commitments during this season. If someone declines, tell them you'll miss them—and leave it at that.

DO: COOK AHEAD AND USE AS MANY PREMADE ITEMS AS YOU'D LIKE.

Using preprepared items will keep you from being stuck in the kitchen all night. Go mingle and have fun with your guests.

DON'T: UNDERESTIMATE THE FOOD AND BEVERAGE BUDGET.

Set aside a few extra dollars if you can—you'll thank yourself later.

DO: PLAN AHEAD IF YOU'LL PLAY SOME GAMES.

Communicate your ideas with folks ahead of time. Some enjoy games, while others would rather watch from the sidelines.

DON'T: FORGET A GREAT PLAYLIST.

Be sure to include a cover of "Rockin' Around the Christmas Tree" by one of your favorite artists (see page 120 for some ideas).

DO: PUT OUT PLENTY OF TRASH CANS.

It's inevitable—folks will ask you where the trash can is. Put a couple in clear sight so that people can take care of their business and get on with the party.

DON'T: STRESS ABOUT MESS.

Your home doesn't have to be spotless to be guest-ready. Just clean where your guests will be, and close off any rooms where they won't be.

DO: MAKE SURE YOU JOIN THE FUN.

Parties are for everyone to enjoy—even the host. Plus, guests will feel free to enjoy themselves more if they see their host having a blast.

DON'T: BE SHY ABOUT ASKING FOR HELP.

Hosting any gathering is a lot. Ask guests to bring dishes or drinks so you don't have to provide so much. And when guests ask if they can help you, say yes! Ask them to wash dishes or help tidy up.

Mistletoe hung where you can see

Decorating *with* MISTLETOE

The Green Plant of Love

Meet me under the mistletoe, the signs and throw pillows say. And we sigh—it's so romantic! We hang the light-green foliage adorned with white berries from our doorways and arches, hoping to smooch our sweetheart or set up a meet-cute trap at a party. But the history of mistletoe wasn't always associated with romance. Rather, it is steeped in myths that date back to ancient times.

In Norse mythology, Balder was the god of peace and began to have dreams that told of his death. His mother, the goddess Frigg, was determined to help her son and made every object in the world promise not to harm him, but she overlooked one thing: mistletoe. The trickster god Loki learned of this oversight and fashioned an arrow made of the green plant. During a game where gods and goddesses would throw objects at Balder to test his mother's protection, the arrow made of mistletoe hit Balder, mortally wounding him. After her son's death, Frigg declared mistletoe to be an object of love, transforming its association as an object of grief to something made of love. She promised to bestow a kiss upon anyone who passed beneath it.

This tradition of being kissed under the mistletoe made its way through Europe and was eventually popularized at Christmas by English servants n the eighteenth century, who would steal a kiss as they stood beneath the plant.

Want to make your own bundle of mistletoe? You can find the real thing growing on other woody plants (it's actually parasitic). Or you could just as easily find a fake version at your local craft store.

So let the spirit of love live on, and meet your sweetheart under the mistletoe.

Cocktail Hour Cheese & Herb Crackers

PREP TIME: 15 MINUTES / TOTAL TIME: 35 MINUTES / MAKES: 30 CRACKERS

You can't eat mistletoe (it's a toxic little beauty), but you can take a cue from its look with these herb-infused crackers garnished with thyme. Fresh (or dried) herbs are combined with rich cheese and baked to a crisp to create the perfect snack for cocktail hour.

1 cup all-purpose flour

1 teaspoon baking powder

1/2 cup butter, cold and cubed

1/2 cup grated cheddar cheese

1/4 cup grated Parmesan cheese

Pinch of salt

Herbes de Provence (optional)

Everything seasoning (optional)

Sprigs of fresh thyme as garnish

DIRECTIONS

1. Preheat the oven to 350 degrees F. Line a cookie sheet with parchment paper.

2. Add the flour, baking powder, cubed butter, cheeses, and a pinch of salt to a food processor and pulse until it forms a dough. If necessary, add a tablespoon of water to help it come together.

3. Roll out the dough onto a floured surface to about 1/2-inch thickness and cut out small 2-inch circles with a cookie cutter. Place on the prepared cookie sheet and sprinkle with herbs or seasoning.

4. Bake for 15 to 20 minutes, until golden brown and hardened. Allow them to cool completely before serving. Garnish with sprigs of thyme if desired.

Mistletoe Magic!

You can adorn any doorway, hallway, or ceiling with this lovely green plant as a piece of decor as much as a love trap. The easiest way to hang is with ribbon, twine, or wire around the stem and then affixing it to a hook or nail.

Make Your Own Mistletoe Wreath

TOTAL TIME: 1 HOUR / MAKES: 1 WREATH

Everyone is familiar with the mistletoe bundles hanging above doorways, but mistletoe makes a beautiful wreath too. Its white berries add a touch of snowy "pop" against the light-green leaves. Leave as is for a neutral feel or add red accents for a more traditional look.

1 premade evergreen wreath; 12 to 16 inches

1 bunch large mistletoe

1 bunch large heather

Helleborus rose flowers

Winterberry holly berries

Pernettya

Rosehips

Floral wire

Wire cutters

INSTRUCTIONS

1. Attach a loop of floral wire to the frame of the evergreen wreath for hanging when finished.

2. Place the larger mistletoe and heather pieces around the wreath, all going in the same direction. Use the floral wire to wrap and secure pieces to the wreath.

3. After the larger pieces are attached, evenly add accent pieces of flowers and berries, also securing with the floral wire.

Frosted Rosé and Rosemary Spritz

TOTAL TIME: 15 MINUTES / SERVES: 6

Elevate your cocktail game with this sophisticated pairing of delicate, floral rosé and aromatic rosemary. It's as visually stunning as it is refreshing. And if you stand with your glass under the mistletoe, you may be even more delighted!

2 cups fresh cranberries, divided

1 cup raw sugar

1 cup water

6 sprigs fresh rosemary, divided

1 bottle sparkling wine

▶ DIRECTIONS

1. Combine 1 cup of the cranberries, raw sugar, water, and half the rosemary in a small saucepan and bring to a boil, stirring occasionally. Reduce the heat and simmer for 10 minutes. Cool and strain mixture into a jar.
2. Fill 6 cocktail glasses with ice. Add 1 tablespoon of the cranberry syrup to each glass and top with sparkling wine.
3. Divide the remaining cranberries and fresh rosemary between the glasses and carefully stir.

MOCKTAIL MOMENT: *You can make this spirit-free but still sparkling with a nonalcoholic sparkling wine or cider. Or substitute Sprite for the alcohol for a carbonated twist.*

Every couple tries to stop

Celebrating Love at CHRISTMAS

When Romance and the Holidays Meet

It's a season with sparks of romance around every corner. Cozy sleigh rides. Snowball fights ending in breathless laughter. Walking hand in hand in the snow. Frosty nights spent snuggling under a blanket by the warm glow of a crackling fire.

Forget Valentine's Day—Christmas is the real season of love. (Want some proof? More engagements happen at Christmastime than any other time of year—including Valentine's Day. Drop that fun fact when you're at the punch bowl . . . or when you need your other half to get a move on and get a ring already!)

We want to spend the Christmas season with the people who are special to us, and our partners are no exception. That's probably why romance is such a huge part of Christmas movie storylines. Hallmark has practically made watching Christmas romance movies its own kind of sport.

In the hustle and bustle of the season, when your calendar fills up and your to-do list grows a mile long, making time to spend a special moment with your special someone can feel a little difficult. You're being pulled in so many directions as it is. But you don't have to be a big-city lawyer who returns to her small town only to find her hunky high school crush running his own bakery to find love this holiday season. Sometimes finding the spark of romance during Christmastime comes when you're on the couch together laughing about holidays past, at a restaurant dreaming about the year ahead, or even in the kitchen cooking a special dish together.

Not every couple has to stop—under the mistletoe—to fan the flame of romance at Christmas. Want some ideas for how to make this holiday special for you and your love? Read on!

Tips for a romantic night in . . .

Create a cozy atmosphere. Dim the lamps, light some candles, and play some soft Christmas music in the background.

Prepare something special in the kitchen. Make a cozy drink like a Gingerbread Espresso Martini (page 55). Set out a charcuterie board or your partner's favorite Christmas treats.

If you have a fireplace, light a fire for some added warmth and ambiance. If you don't, a virtual fireplace on your TV can also make a room feel cozy.

Watch old movie favorites to bring the warmth of nostalgia into the evening. Bring some plush pillows and a cozy throw blanket into the mix.

Wrap gifts together. Put on a playlist and enjoy some time talking about what you're giving your loved ones.

Tips for a romantic night out . . .

Head to a neighborhood in town known for spectacular light displays. Walk hand in hand as you take in the sparkling lights.

Visit a winter wonderland with fun activities like sleigh rides, bonfires, ice skating, and more.

Walk through a Christmas market. Browse the stalls, sip on mulled wine, and sample festive treats as you shop for unique gifts.

Attend a Christmas concert or show. Or you might enjoy a production of *The Nutcracker* ballet.

Gaze at the stars. If the sky is clear, bundle up and step outside to stargaze together. Don't forget to bring a thermos of hot cocoa!

COUPLES' CHRISTMAS QUIZ

This game is a blast to play with other couples. Each person answers questions about their partner on a piece of paper. Whichever couple has the most points wins! Get ready for a few laughs along the way.

- Favorite childhood memory at Christmastime?
- Real or artificial tree?
- Favorite Christmas movie?
- Most annoying Christmas song?
- Best Christmas gift they've ever received?
- Weirdest Christmas tradition in their family?
- The Christmas treat or dessert they look forward to most?
- Favorite ornament on the tree?
- Who's the better gift wrapper: you or them?
- Who's the better gift giver: you or them?
- The most over-the-top thing they do for Christmas?
- Their go-to Christmas drink?
- A celebrity they would invite to Christmas dinner?
- Character from *A Christmas Carol* they are most like?
- Favorite place to spend the holidays?

Luscious Chocolate Mousse

TOTAL TIME: 15 MINUTES / SERVES: 4

Looking for a rich, velvety dessert for a night in with your sweetheart? Snuggle under a blanket and share a cup of creamy chocolate mousse as you watch a holiday movie.

FOR THE WHIPPED CREAM

1/2 cup heavy whipping cream

1 tablespoon powdered sugar

1 teaspoon vanilla extract

1/4 teaspoon salt

FOR THE MOUSSE

2 cups heavy whipping cream

1/2 cup cocoa powder

2/3 cup powdered sugar

1/2 teaspoon vanilla extract

1/4 teaspoon salt

Semisweet chocolate bar, grated

▶ TO MAKE THE WHIPPED CREAM

1. In the bowl of a stand mixer fitted with the whisk attachment, or in a bowl using a hand mixer, whip the heavy cream on medium speed until frothy.
2. Add the powdered sugar, vanilla, and salt. Mix on low until incorporated, then increase speed to medium until stiff peaks form.
3. Transfer to a separate bowl and store in the refrigerator until ready to serve.

▶ TO MAKE THE MOUSSE

1. In the same mixing bowl, whip the heavy cream on medium speed until thick and frothy.

2. Stop the mixer and sift in the cocoa and powdered sugar. Add the vanilla, then beat again on low speed until cocoa and powdered sugar are mostly incorporated.

3. Increase the mixer speed back to medium and whip until medium peaks form. Portion the mousse into dessert cups.

4. To serve, top each cup with the whipped cream and finish with grated chocolate.

Gingerbread Espresso Martini

PREP TIME: 10 MINUTES / TOTAL TIME: 15 MINUTES / SERVES: 2

Add a little spice to your espresso martini with the warm flavors of gingerbread. The perfect way to balance rich coffee flavors with seasonal cheer!

FOR THE GINGERBREAD SYRUP

2 tablespoons light molasses

2 tablespoons honey

1/2 cup firmly packed brown sugar

2/3 cup water

1 teaspoon ground ginger

1/4 teaspoon ground allspice

2 cinnamon sticks

FOR TWO MARTINIS

2 gingerbread cookies, crushed into fine crumbs

4 ounces vodka

2 ounces coffee liqueur

2 ounces espresso

2 ounces gingerbread syrup

▶ TO MAKE THE SYRUP

In a small saucepan, combine all ingredients over medium heat. Cook, stirring occasionally, for 5 minutes. Turn off heat and let cool.

▶ TO MAKE THE MARTINIS

1. Place the gingerbread cookie crumbs on a plate. Dip the rim of each glass in the cooled gingerbread syrup, then dip in the gingerbread cookie crumbs.
2. Add vodka, coffee liqueur, espresso, and gingerbread syrup to a large cocktail shaker. Fill with ice and shake for 30 seconds.
3. Strain the cocktail into the prepared martini glasses and enjoy.

Rockin' around
the Christmas tree

An Ode to ORNAMENTS

Make the Season Sparkle with Splendor

You can't rock around a Christmas tree without admiring the ornaments. What would a holiday tree be without these colorful, shiny seasonal pieces?

Pulling out your box of Christmas ornaments is thrilling, isn't it? Lifting the lid and picking up ornaments that have sparkled on your tree for years, or even decades, can feel like saying hello to an old friend. Look, there's your "Baby's First Christmas" ornament that your grandma embroidered. There's your gap-toothed kindergarten smile, stuck on a piece of red construction paper in the shape of a tree. There's the fine silver bell that your father gave your mother for the ten-year anniversary of the first Christmas they spent together—the bell she forbade you to touch because she knew you might break it. The colorful baubles, the wooden nutcrackers, the Christmas pickle you can't wait to hide on the tree—they're all snug inside the box, ready for you to hang and admire for another holiday season.

Folks have been hanging ornaments on Christmas trees since the sixteenth century, when Germans began adorning their trees with fruits, nuts, and other edible items. Over the years perishable ornaments gave way to intricate items handmade from wood or glass, and today there are ornaments to suit every style and taste. These days decorating a Christmas tree can seem like an extension of your personality, where you show off your

unique taste and the ornaments that are special to you. Maybe you grew up in Wisconsin, and your tree is filled with Green Bay Packers ornaments. Maybe you're a foodie who has a whole tree filled with ornaments of your favorite foods. Maybe you're not picky about how your tree is decorated at all, and you fill the branches with a random assortment. Maybe your tree shows the ornaments you've collected through the years—small items and moments that add up to reflect a life of love and a style all your own.

Ornaments tell a story—*your* story.

Christmas Ornament Variations

Use ornaments in various themes to create lots of different Christmas tree vibes.

- Choose ornaments in one or two colors to create a striking, coordinated palette.
- Choose a few shapes (that aren't baubles) to create a different but cohesive look.
- Choose to decorate your tree with a particular location in mind. Look for ornaments with a nautical, tropical, or desert theme.
- Into Christmas movies? Find ornaments with your favorite characters for a pop culture tree.
- If you're a foodie, you'd probably love to display your favorites on a tree filled with food ornaments.
- You could use ornaments all made of the same material. For example, felt ornaments in the same color palette lend a handmade look to a tree.

SO MANY WAYS TO HANG YOUR ORNAMENTS

Ornaments don't just belong on a Christmas tree. You can hang them plenty of places inside and out so you can enjoy them everywhere.

- Give ornaments plenty of room to hang apart from others so folks can take them in.
- Display them over a window so you can enjoy them when you're not near the tree.
- Create your own mobile to display ornaments wherever you'd like.
- Let your neighbors enjoy your decor—hang large ornaments on a tree outdoors.

Pro Tip: To make your own icing, mix 3 cups powdered sugar with 4 to 5 tablespoons milk, adding one tablespoon at a time until desired consistency. Tint with food coloring of your choice.

Christmas Ornament Cookies

PREP TIME: 15 MINUTES / TOTAL TIME: 5 1/2 HOURS / MAKES: 24 COOKIES

These charming treats are not only delicious—they can double as decor for the tree. Display these at a party on a display stand or mini tree for an extra fun effect.

1 cup butter, softened

1 cup granulated sugar

1 egg, beaten

1 teaspoon vanilla extract

2 1/2 cups all-purpose flour

1/2 teaspoon salt

Cookie icing, red and green or any preferred color

DIRECTIONS

1. In the bowl of a stand mixer, cream the butter and sugar together. Add the egg and vanilla and continue to beat until just incorporated.
2. Add in the flour and salt and mix until dough forms. Shape the dough into a ball, wrap in plastic wrap, and chill in the refrigerator for 4 hours.
3. Preheat the oven to 350 degrees F. Prepare a cookie sheet with parchment paper.
4. Roll out the dough onto a floured surface to 1/4-inch thickness. Cut the dough with ornament or other holiday cookie cutters and place on the prepared cookie sheet.
5. Bake for 8 to 10 minutes or until the cookies are just beginning to turn golden. Let the cookies cool completely on a wire rack.
6. Using the cookie icing, decorate the cookies as desired. Let dry until hardened, about 1 hour.

DIY Felt Gingerbread Man Ornament

TOTAL TIME: 2 HOURS / MAKES: 1 ORNAMENT

Play up the vintage vibes on your tree with this felt gingerbread man ornament. Easy to make, this craft is perfect to do with kids on a snowy day—or to keep your hands busy during a Christmas movie marathon.

Cardboard for template

Scissors

Brown and red felt fabric

Red-and-white checkered ribbon

Sewing needle

Black thread

Red embroidery floss

Glue gun and glue sticks

Polyester fiberfill

Red ribbon, 1/4-inch wide, approximately 6 inches long

▶ INSTRUCTIONS

1. Draw the shape of a gingerbread man onto the cardboard, either by using a template or tracing a cookie cutter, and then cut the shape out.

2. Trace around the cardboard cutout onto brown felt fabric twice, once for the back and once for the front. Cut both shapes out of the fabric.

3. On one of the two pieces, sew "buttons" for eyes using black thread.

4. Out of red felt fabric, cut a smile and 2 small round buttons.

5. For the bow tie, cut a small piece out of the checkered ribbon. Wrap red embroidery floss around the center of the fabric and tie off.

6. With a hot glue gun, attach the mouth, bow tie, and buttons to the front piece.

7. Using a blanket stitch and red embroidery floss, sew all around the outside of the gingerbread man, attaching the front and back pieces but leaving a small opening at the top of the head to fill with fiberfill.

8. Fill the gingerbread man with the desired amount of fiberfill.

9. Using the red ribbon, make a loop for hanging and insert it in the top of the head, then finish sewing the gingerbread man closed using the red floss and blanket stitch.

Pro Tip:

If you would rather use a plastic fillable ornament or other container for display, make sure it is made from safe, food-grade material.

Christmas Salad Balls

PREP TIME: 10 MINUTES / TOTAL TIME: 20 MINUTES / SERVES: 12

What a striking way to serve the salad at your holiday party? Serve your salad in a glass ornament bauble! Your guests will never forget this unique offering.

1 pound smoked ham, cut into bite-size pieces

1 pound smoked turkey, cut into bite-size pieces

2 cups lettuce, like mâche or butter lettuce

1 cup microgreens

12 pepperoncini peppers, cored and sliced

2 shallots, sliced thin

1 cup grape tomatoes, halved

2 tablespoons champagne vinegar

6 tablespoons extra virgin olive oil

Kosher salt to taste

Freshly ground black pepper to taste

12 glass terrarium balls

DIRECTIONS

1. In a large mixing bowl, combine the ham, turkey, lettuce, microgreens, pepperoncini, shallots, and tomatoes.
2. Drizzle the vinegar and oil over the salad and season to taste with salt and pepper. Toss the salad until coated.
3. Divide the salad equally between the balls and hang them on a tree or other display.

Let the Christmas
spirit ring

Getting *into the* CHRISTMAS SPIRIT

Embrace the Magic of the Holidays

There's something truly special about Christmas spirit. Joy and peace and love feel palpable this time of year. People are a little kinder, a little more willing to lend a helping hand. Generosity overflows not only at the dining table but also in the community kitchens, the Salvation Army kettles, the gifts for a kid who wouldn't otherwise have much to unwrap. Those are the values we love to see moving through the world this time of year, whether it's in our lives or in the movies and stories we hold dear. (There's a reason Ebenezer Scrooge's story has been told every holiday season for nearly 150 years—we love a Christmas season heart-warmer.)

There are all kinds of things that usher us into the Christmas season and make our spirits bright:

- Things you **see**, like Christmas trees and decorations
- Things you **hear**, like classic carols, songs, and stories
- Things you **smell**, like a fresh fir tree or spicy cinnamon rolls baking in the oven
- Things you **feel**, like the cold nipping at your nose as your footsteps crunch through the snow
- Things you **taste**, like your grandma's pineapple Christmas ham or a batch of chocolate fudge

But perhaps most of all, getting into the Christmas spirit happens when we make connections to the people around us, whether we're giving away a tin of peppermint bark to our beloved mail carrier or sharing a laugh or two over a Cranberry Sleigh Ride Cocktail (page 77) with a friend. Sharing the joy and love of the season with those around us is the best gift we could ever give or receive.

Pro Tip: You can buy pre-crushed peppermints or have fun with your kids by crushing mints in a resealable plastic bag.

Fudgy Peppermint Squares

PREP TIME: 15 MINUTES / TOTAL TIME: 1 1/2 HOURS / SERVES: 32

This seasonal favorite is a great gift to give away this time of year. Pick up some festive tins from the dollar store, fill them with bark, and hand them out to teachers, delivery drivers, friends, or anyone who would enjoy this shareable treat. (And because it's gluten-free, this is a good option for people you're still getting to know.)

2 cups dark or semisweet chocolate, coarsely chopped

6 tablespoons heavy cream

1 teaspoon peppermint extract

2 cups good quality white chocolate, coarsely chopped

30 hard peppermint candies, crushed

DIRECTIONS

1. Line a 9 x 13-inch baking pan with parchment paper.
2. Melt the dark chocolate, heavy cream, and peppermint extract in the top half of a double boiler over just barely simmering water. Stirring constantly, scrape down the sides of the pot with a rubber spatula. Pour or spread the melted chocolate into the bottom of the prepared pan. Let chill in the refrigerator until firm, about 15 to 20 minutes.
3. Melt the white chocolate in the top of the double boiler over barely simmering water, stirring constantly, just until melted. Quickly pour the melted white chocolate over the chilled chocolate layer and spread evenly.
4. Sprinkle with crushed peppermints. Refrigerate until completely firm, about 30 minutes.
5. Cut into small squares to serve. Store in an airtight container in the refrigerator for up to two weeks.

Cookie Baking Mix in a Jar

TOTAL TIME TO ASSEMBLE: 15 MINUTES / MAKES: 1 JAR (12 COOKIES)

One of the best ways to let the Christmas spirit ring is to give away a homemade dessert gift—without cooking a single thing!

FOR THE COOKIES

1/3 cup butter, room temperature

1 large egg

1/2 teaspoon vanilla extract

FOR THE GIFT JAR

1/2 cup all-purpose flour

1/2 cup whole wheat flour

1/2 teaspoon salt

1/2 teaspoon baking soda

1/4 cup granulated sugar

1/4 cup raw sugar

1/4 cup dried sweetened cranberries

1/4 cup dark chocolate chips

▶ TO MAKE THE COOKIES

1. Preheat oven to 350 degrees F.
2. Add butter, egg, and vanilla to a mixing bowl; beat on high until smooth.
3. Reduce the mixing speed to medium and slowly add all of the ingredients in the jar. Mix until well blended.
4. Scoop tablespoons of the cookie dough onto a prepared cookie sheet. Bake for 10 to 12 minutes or until the edges of the cookies are lightly golden brown and the tops are set.
5. Remove the cookies from the oven and allow them to cool .

TO ASSEMBLE THE GIFT JAR

1. In a 16-ounce mason jar, layer the flour, wheat flour, salt, baking soda, and sugars. Add the cranberries and chocolate chips.

2. Tightly secure the lid on the jar, decorate as desired, and add a note with directions for preparing the cookies.

Cranberry Sleigh Ride Cocktail

TOTAL TIME: 5 MINUTES / SERVES: 1

Toast the holidays with this tart blend of cranberries and festive flavors. This seasonal sip will be making spirits bright, indeed.

2 ounces amaretto

2 ounces cranberry juice

½ lime

2 sugared cranberries for garnish

DIRECTIONS

1. Pour the amaretto and cranberry juice into a cocktail shaker filled with ice. Squeeze in the juice of half a lime. Cover and shake for 15 seconds.
2. Strain the cocktail into a stylish glass and garnish with speared sugared cranberries.

Pro Tip:

To make sugared cranberries, bring ½ cup water and ½ cup sugar to a boil in a small saucepan. Remove from heat and add 1 cup fresh cranberries. Let sit for 10 minutes. Remove cranberries from the syrup and dry on parchment paper for an hour. Roll the cranberries on a plate with ¼ cup sugar until coated. Let dry. Store in a lidded container on the countertop.

Instant Christmas Vibes

Want to infuse the Christmas spirit into your home, like, *right now*? Think about your five senses: the things you see, hear, feel, smell, and taste. Sprinkle a bit of the holidays in each of those areas, and pretty soon it'll begin to feel a lot like Christmas.

Things you can see: Add small touches of the season to your home, like a pine bough on your door or windowsill. Use fairy lights to bring soft lighting to your space.

Things you can hear: Turn on a Christmas album or playlist you love. Listen to the logs crackling in the fireplace or play a YouTube video of a crackling log on your TV.

Things you can feel: Put on soft fabrics like wool, fleece, and cashmere. Wear fuzzy socks and oversized sweaters. Snuggle under a cozy throw blanket.

Things you can smell: Light scented candles to bring in smells of vanilla, cinnamon, or pine. Make a batch of stovetop potpourri or gingerbread cookies.

Things you can taste: Make a cup of warm, spicy Christmas tea or hot cocoa (page 109). Pull a buttery cookie out of the tin.

Gift Wrapping Fun

Gift wrapping doesn't have to be a chore! Use these ideas to make the minutes tick by.

- **Create a wrapping station.** Gather all the wrapping supplies you need: paper, ribbons, tags, scissors, tape. Remember to grab a pen too.
- **Play something festive.** Put on your favorite Christmas music playlist or a Christmas-themed episode of your favorite podcast.
- **Invite friends and loved ones to join you.** Just make sure you wrap *their* gifts another time.
- **Grab something yummy to drink.** Hot cocoa, mulled wine, a Christmas cocktail—any festive drink to enjoy while you work.
- **Get creative with wrapping materials.** Try newspaper, maps, or cloth. Add small accessories like twigs, pinecones, or sprigs of holly.
- **Use gift-wrap designs that make you smile.** Whether it's dogs, dinosaurs, or your favorite Christmas movie characters, wrapping gifts with unexpected designs will bring some joy.

Later we'll have some pumpkin pie

Yummy CHRISTMAS Sweets

Savor the Sweetness of the Season

What is it about Christmas that makes us want to crank up the oven and bake? Maybe because we welcome a warm kitchen with hot, fresh treats when it's cold outside. Or perhaps we're looking for a snack as sweet as the season. Maybe it's a combination of both. Christmas has always been a season to indulge, and no holiday is complete without a sugar rush.

Cookie parties. Christmas fudge. Yule logs and puddings and fruitcakes. Cultures around the world welcome in the holiday with treats that have long-standing traditions and generations of memories for families everywhere.

Food is one of the great connectors in our world. The act of making and sharing a treat with someone can turn a stranger into a friend, turn back the clock to a simpler time, or turn an ordinary moment into something a little magical. Food reminds us that we're not quite so different from each other, that we all enjoy moments when we can lay down our work and nourish ourselves with a bit of food and conversation. And when we make the pumpkin pie our mother whipped together every holiday or the fudge our grandpa loved to sneak from the tin, we say hello to the memories that made our seasons and made us who we are. A little butter and sugar can do a lot.

So this Christmas season, let's get into the kitchen and make some magic!

Brenda Lee's Praline Pumpkin Pie

Reprinted from Brenda's Cookbook: Hits from the Kitchen, *courtesy of Brenda Lee.*

PREP TIME: 30 MINUTES / TOTAL TIME: 2 HOURS / SERVES: 8 TO 10

"Later we'll have some pumpkin pie" *. . . well, later is now! You won't be able to stop humming the song as you make this family favorite recipe from Brenda's own collection.*

1/4 cup butter, melted

1/2 cup sugar

1 cup pecans, chopped

1 envelope unflavored gelatin

1/2 cup cold water

3/4 cup packed brown sugar

1 (1 lb.) can pumpkin (not pumpkin pie mix)

1/4 cup milk

1/2 teaspoon salt

1 teaspoon cinnamon

1 teaspoon freshly grated nutmeg

1/4 teaspoon ground allspice

1 cup heavy cream, whipped

1 (10-inch) pie shell, baked

▶ DIRECTIONS

1. Mix the butter, sugar, and chopped pecans in a small skillet and sauté over medium heat, stirring until golden, 3 or 4 minutes. Turn onto foil or waxed paper to cool. Crumble.

2. Mix the gelatin with the water in a small saucepan. Place over medium heat and stir until dissolved. Remove from the heat.

3. Add the brown sugar, then mix in the pumpkin, milk, and spices. Fold in the whipped cream.

4. Place 1/2 of the crumbled pecan mixture into the bottom of the baked pie shell. Add the filling and refrigerate until pie is set, then add the remaining pecan mixture to the top for garnish. Serve with a dollop of real whipped cream.

Christmas Tiramisu

PREP TIME: 30 MINUTES / TOTAL TIME: 4 1/2 HOURS / SERVES: 10

If pumpkin pie is more of a Thanksgiving dessert in your family, try a Christmas tiramisu instead. The peppermint in the candy canes smooths out the rich white chocolate, while pomegranate pieces add sparkling ruby reds to this holiday delight.

8 ounces mascarpone cheese

1½ cups heavy cream

2 tablespoons powdered sugar

¾ teaspoon peppermint extract, divided

1 cup espresso or strongly brewe coffee, cooled

4 tablespoons chocolate liqueur

2 tablespoons granulated sugar

1 package ladyfinger cookies (about 20)

1 tablespoon unsweetened cocoa for dusting

2 tablespoons dark chocolate, grated

3 candy canes, crushed

¼ cup pomegranate seeds

10 small candy canes for garnish

▶ DIRECTIONS

1. In a medium-sized bowl, add the mascarpone, heavy cream, powdered sugar, and ½ teaspoon of peppermint extract; beat with an electric mixer until soft peaks form.

2. In a small bowl, combine the espresso, chocolate liqueur, granulated sugar, and ¼ teaspoon of peppermint extract.

3. Briefly dip each ladyfinger into the coffee mixture, then place it in the bottom of a 9 x 7-inch rectangular baking dish. Repeat until there is a full, even layer of ladyfingers.

4. Place the cream mixture into a pastry bag and pipe about half of it over the layer of ladyfingers.

5. Add a second layer of coffee-dipped ladyfingers and pipe the remaining cream mixture on top.

6. Dust with the cocoa followed by the grated chocolate, then sprinkle with the crushed candy cane pieces and pomegranate seeds. Refrigerate for at least 4 hours before serving. Garnish each slice (or dish) with a whole candy cane before serving.

HOST A GINGERBREAD HOUSE COMPETITION

Who says that sugar can't be part of the fun? Bring out the festive (and maybe a little feisty) holiday spirit by hosting a friendly gingerbread house decorating competition with your friends and loved ones.

Once you've decided what materials are acceptable to use and who will be judging your creations, get building! Working in groups of two to four decorators will ensure everyone has something to do. If there are children in your decorating group, perhaps designate more structural tasks and fine motor work like piping to the older decorators, while younger hands might enjoy placing candies and other decorative items onto the display.

Judge's score sheet

SCORE 1 TO 10 FOR EACH

FOR CREATIVITY AND ORIGINALITY __________

Is there anything new or innovative about the house's design or decoration?

FOR ATTENTION TO DETAIL __________

Does it have intricate touches that add character to the scene?

FOR DIFFICULTY LEVEL __________

Were complex techniques used to construct or decorate the house?

FOR STABILITY AND STRUCTURE __________

How sturdy is the construction of the house?

FOR OVERALL APPEARANCE __________

Consider the visual impact of the gingerbread house. Is it striking? Attractive?

TOTAL POINTS: __________

Host a Dessert Party!

The holidays are a great excuse for a sugar rush. Instead of serving a dinner, why not host a dessert party? Each guest can bring their favorite treat to share. You'll want to provide a neutral beverage like coffee, tea, or milk to accompany the sweets.

To ensure each guest brings a different kind of dessert, create a list for your guests to choose from: cake, pie, cookies, dessert bars, bark, brownies, and more. Use an app or gather your guests on a simple text chain to make it easy for folks to claim their dessert.

CREATE A CHRISTMAS COOKIE DECORATION STATION

While you're playing host, your guests can have fun dressing up cookies with a flair of their own. Here's a checklist of items to have at your decoration station:

- ☐ Piping bags and piping tips
- ☐ White frosting and lots of food coloring
- ☐ Plenty of small dishes to hold your colored frosting
- ☐ Candies and nibbles for decoration: candy canes, chocolate kisses, chopped nuts, red and green sprinkles

Merry and Bright Idea

Running short on time? Pick up ready-made cookie dough at the store. No one will know—or care—when they're decorating their sugar cookie or gingerbread person.

And we'll do some caroling

Singing Through the SEASON

Spreading Christmas Cheer Through Song

Say the word *caroling* and you might picture a group of carolers going out to sing on a cold, dark night dressed in capes and hoopskirts and pipe hats like in a Dickens novel. But did you know the caroling tradition is older than *A Christmas Carol*? Like, *centuries* older?

The term *carol* usually refers to a Christmas song of religious origin. Some scholars trace Christian hymns back to fourth-century Rome, where they were sung in Latin. However, in the thirteenth century, St. Francis of Assisi encouraged the development of Christmas songs in singers' native languages, so every person could understand and enjoy the lyrics.

Fun Fact!

Some of the oldest carols we still enjoy today are "Good King Wenceslas" and "The Holly and the Ivy," both of which were composed in the Middle Ages.

Over the next few centuries, the existence of Christmas hymns in European languages grew, and a carol revival in the eighteenth century strengthened the tradition of singing them at Christmastime.

Fun Fact!

In 1857 "Jingle Bells" was written and composed by James Lord Pierpont. The song was originally called "One Horse Open Sleigh" and was not received well by listeners of the day.

Many sang these Christmas hymns to keep their spirits up amid the harsh weather and dark nights of winter. (Ever heard the carol "In the Bleak Midwinter"? Yep, that's where it comes from.) By the Victorian period, groups of "wassailers" would walk from door to door during the Christmas season, and as a reward for their efforts to bring cheer in the cold, they were offered a cup of hot, spiced wassail. (The word *wassail* comes from the Old Norse *ves heill*, meaning "be well and in good health.")

So what makes a Christmas carol? While traditionally only a song with religious significance would make the cut, today we consider any song that brings Christmas cheer to be a carol. So send a text to the group chat, make a batch of wassail, and raise your voice to spread some Christmas cheer—even if you're a little off-key.

Spiced Nuts

TOTAL TIME: 1 HOUR / SERVES: 16

This is the perfect snack to take with you while you go caroling. Enjoy the scent of warm spices like cinnamon and nutmeg wafting through your house while the nuts roast.

4 cups mixed unsalted nuts, like cashews, almonds, and pecans

1/4 cup packed brown sugar

2 tablespoons white sugar

1 teaspoon paprika

2 teaspoons ground cinnamon

1/2 teaspoon cayenne pepper

1/2 teaspoon kosher salt

1 egg white

1 tablespoon water

▶ DIRECTIONS

1. Preheat oven to 350 degrees F. Line a cookie sheet with parchment paper.

2. Spread the mixed nuts in an even layer and bake for 10 minutes. Remove the cookie sheet from the oven. Reduce temperature to 325 degrees F.

3. In a small bowl, combine both sugars, paprika, cinnamon, cayenne, and salt.

4. In a large bowl, beat the egg white and water until frothy. Add the mixed nuts to the mixture and toss to coat. Sprinkle in

the spice mixture and toss until completely coated.

5. Spread the nuts in an even layer on the same cookie sheet and return to the oven, stirring occasionally, until the coating is set, 15 to 20 minutes.

6. Remove from the oven and let the nuts cool, about 15 minutes. Separate them with a fork as they cool. Store in a sealed container.

Outdoor Winter Garden Party

If you're caroling during the day, plan an outdoor winter garden party afterward. Make sure these action items are on your checklist:

- Set up a fire in the fire pit for your guests to warm up when they get back.
- Make sure plenty of blankets are on hand.
- Hand out hot drinks to guests, like wassail, mulled wine, hot cocoa, or coffee.
- Set up a soup or chili bar. Keep in a slow cooker to keep it warm outdoors.
- Light some candles and hang string lights, in case the party goes into the night.

Winter Wassail

TOTAL TIME: 30 MINUTES / SERVES: 8

You have a few options for enjoying this delicious, spice-filled beverage. You could make it on the stovetop and carry it with you in a thermos while you're out caroling on a crisp winter evening. Or you could assemble the ingredients in a slow cooker so the flavors meld together and the mixture is piping hot by the time you return. Either way, you win.

8 cups apple cider

4 tablespoons brown sugar

4 cinnamon sticks, plus additional for garnish

½ teaspoon whole cloves

½ teaspoon whole allspice

1 star anise pod

1 orange, sliced

8 ounces spiced rum, optional

▶ DIRECTIONS

1. Place the cider, brown sugar, and cinnamon sticks in a medium pot or slow cooker and mix together. Add cloves, allspice, star anise pod, and orange slices and turn heat to low.

2. Let simmer for about 20 minutes (or several hours in a slow-cooker). Stir in the rum if using.

3. Carefully discard the cinnamon sticks and orange slices. Ladle the mulled cider into mugs, straining out the spices with a fine-mesh strainer. Garnish with a cinnamon stick.

Try This: Leave out the alcohol to make this family-friendly.

You will get a sentimental feeling
Happy Holidays

Remembering CHRISTMASES of Old

Honor the Past and Present

Ask ten people how their family celebrates the Christmas season, and you'll get ten wildly different answers.

If you asked someone from Mexico, they might tell you that they celebrate *Las Posadas*, which commemorates the journey Mary and Joseph took to Bethlehem, and how much they look forward to eating their mom's tamales at Christmas. Ask a Swede, and they might describe attending a St. Lucia's service, a festival of lights that marks the beginning of the Christmas season in Scandinavia on December 13. Germans might describe shopping in nighttime Christmas markets, finding gifts and ornaments for loved ones and getting delicious treats from the stalls. Those hailing from India might share about the Christmas balls and social dances that fill their calendars during the season.

The Christmases of our past inform the holidays we have today, thanks to rich traditions our families and loved ones pass down to us. We get a kick out of eating cinnamon rolls every Christmas morning or going to a candlelight service every Christmas Eve because, in a way, these moments serve as portals to our past. When we open the oven door and slather the sweet cream cheese icing on our rolls, we might remember how our grandmother used to pile on more icing with a wink. When we walk into the church and light a candle, we remember the person we were as we held similar candles in years past.

Christmas is a season of remembering, of celebrating who we were and where we are today. That's one of the most special things about the holiday: the way it tethers us to the past and gives us an opportunity to look at how far we've come across the changing years.

DISPLAY YOUR CHRISTMAS CARDS WITH STYLE

Displaying Christmas cards can add a personal touch to your holiday decor. Here are some creative ways to showcase them at home:

String and clothespins. Stretch twine or ribbon across a wall, door, fireplace, or window. Use mini clothespins to hang the cards.

Card wreath. Create a wreath using a wire or foam base, then attach the cards with clothespins, tape, or clips. Or use a premade wreath or garland and tuck the cards into the branches.

Ladder display. Do you have a ladder in your home, maybe in a foyer or library? Hang cards on the rungs.

Photo holder or wire grid. Use a photo holder or a wire grid display stand to hold your cards. Secure the cards with clips or small clothespins.

Styled shelves. Place the cards in the background of styled shelves for a more muted display.

Picture frames. Place cards inside picture frames for a formal display.

Card tree. Use twine to string cards onto a twig card tree.

Doorframe or staircase. Tape or clip the cards along the edges of a doorframe or the railing of a staircase. Use festive washi tape or decorative clips for added holiday spirit.

Magazine holder or basket. Keep cards handy as you lounge in the living room or den using a basket or magazine holder. You could even display cards on the coffee table so guests can browse through them.

Brioche Bread Pudding with Warm Vanilla Sauce

PREP TIME: 10 MINUTES / TOTAL TIME: 1 HOUR / SERVES: 8

This dessert dates back to the eleventh century, when Europeans mixed together a custard that turned stale bread into a delicious dish. Baked with buttery brioche and topped with vanilla sauce, this bread pudding is a favorite, no matter the crowd—or the century.

1 loaf brioche bread (16 ounces), cubed

4 eggs

2 egg yolks

3 tablespoons butter

2½ cups whole milk

1 cup heavy cream

¾ cup granulated sugar

2 teaspoons vanilla extract

¼ teaspoon salt

2 tablespoons powdered sugar

1 cup raisins or dried fruit

▶ DIRECTIONS

1. Preheat oven to 350 degrees F. Spray a medium casserole dish with cooking spray and arrange the bread cubes in the dish.

2. In a medium bowl, beat the eggs and egg yolks together. In a large saucepan over medium-low heat, combine the butter, milk, cream, sugar, vanilla, and salt. Whisk the eggs into the milk mixture. Continue whisking until the sugar is dissolved, about 3 minutes.

3. Carefully pour the cream mixture evenly over the bread cubes, reserving

1 cup. Transfer the cream-soaked bread cubes to the oven and bake for 35 to 40 minutes, until golden.

4. Return the remaining sauce back to the stove over low heat while whisking so the sauce does not overheat. Whisk until the sauce thickens, about 5 minutes.

5. To serve, pour the thickened sauce over the bread pudding, dust with powdered sugar, and top with the dried fruit.

Pro Tip:

Try dried blueberries or cranberries in place of raisins for a flavorful kick!

Pro Tip: It is important to keep the temperature low when warming the milk to avoid scalding it. Patience is the key here. You don't want that burnt taste to ruin your masterpiece!

Hot Chocolate with Marshmallows

PREP TIME: 15 MINUTES / TOTAL TIME: 30 MINUTES / SERVES: 4

You know it. You love it. And so does everyone else. This classic hot chocolate is perfect on repeat, whether you take it to a holiday party, carry it in a thermos during caroling, or sip it in an oversized mug as you snuggle on the couch on a chilly evening. marshmallows are always encouraged.

- $1\frac{1}{2}$ cups mini marshmallows
- 4 cups whole milk
- $\frac{1}{4}$ cup granulated sugar
- 1 teaspoon vanilla extract
- $\frac{1}{4}$ cup unsweetened cocoa
- 2 ounces semisweet chocolate, chopped, plus 1 tablespoon grated
- 4 candy canes, optional

▶ DIRECTIONS

1. Spread the marshmallows in a single layer on a cookie sheet and place them under the broiler for 1 to 2 minutes, until just golden. Remove from oven and set aside.

2. Add milk, sugar, vanilla, and cocoa to a saucepan and cook over medium-low heat, whisking until milk is warmed through, about 5 minutes.

3. Add the chopped chocolate and continue to whisk until the chocolate is completely melted. Be patient—this can take 5 minutes or more.

4. Remove from heat and carefully pour the hot chocolate into mugs. Top with marshmallows and grated chocolate. Add a candy cane to each if desired.

Handmade Christmas Cards

TOTAL TIME: 1 HOUR

Make your own Christmas cards or ornaments that can be shared and hung for years to come.

White cardstock

Variety of holiday cookie cutters

Pencil

Eraser

Variety of colorful acrylic craft paint

Variety of colorful ink pads

Alphabet and holiday-themed stamps

Cotton swabs

Small round foam paintbrushes

Fine-tip black marker

Glue gun and glue sticks

Variety of trimmings for decoration

▶ INSTRUCTIONS

1. Cut cardstock into various sizes from gift tag or oversized cards, or purchase premeasured and precut blank cards and tags.

2. Using a pencil, trace a faint outline of a cookie cutter shape as a guide. Alternatively, use an alphabet or holiday stamp or sketch a basic shape using a pencil or black marker.

3. With a paint-covered fingertip, cotton swab, paint brush, flat end of a pencil, or a mix of the tools, dot the paint in desired colors and patterns onto the drawn design, dipping into more paint as needed.

4. Once dried, erase any remaining visible pencil marks if needed.

5. Apply any desired lettering using the stamps, pads, and black marker.

6. Using a hot glue gun, carefully affix any remaining trimmings, such as ribbons or bows. Get creative with the finishing touches.

Merry and Bright Idea

Make sure to display heartfelt ornaments and decorations around your house. The joy you'll get from seeing these memories from the past is unparalleled.

When you hear voices singing, "let's be jolly"

Bringing Joy

to the

WORLD

Modern Christmas Songs We Love

The grocery store. Your dentist's waiting room. The aisles of Target. Aunt Cathy's house. Ready or not, everywhere you go from November 1 to December 25, the soundtrack of Christmas will be playing to give your ears a full-on holiday hug.

For seven weeks out of the year, we make an agreement that these songs, many coming from the 1940s to 1960s, will be our collective soundtrack. Perhaps we like the novelty they bring because they sound so different from the rest of the music we listen to, or perhaps we welcome the nostalgia they provide. We crave familiarity and comfort this time of year. And it seems the rules of popular music are reversed at Christmastime—it's pretty hard for a newer artist to break into becoming part of the Christmas music canon because we hang on tight to our favorite classics. Except for Mariah Carey—because she's Mariah Carey.

When it comes to Christmas music, we expect to hear sleigh bells. We expect harmonies. We love upbeat melodies and soft ballads in equal measure. And who doesn't adore a lush orchestra with a big sound?

Whether you dig out your records or curate the perfect Spotify playlist, it's time to celebrate the songs we all know and love.

Fun Fact!

When do Americans start listening to Christmas music? According to Spotify streaming data, there's a small bump in Christmas music streams starting November 1, but the surge grows much larger right after Thanksgiving.

Rockin' Around the Christmas Tree Cake Pops

PREP TIME: 2 HOURS / TOTAL TIME: 3 1/2 HOURS / MAKES: 36 CAKE POPS

Add a festive twist to your holiday table with these bite-sized Christmas trees. Perfect for parties, these cake pops are as fun to make as they are to eat.

1 box vanilla cake mix

$\frac{1}{4}$ cup vegetable oil

$\frac{1}{4}$ cup butter, softened

1 cup powdered sugar

1 teaspoon vanilla extract

1 teaspoon milk

4 cups green candy melts

36 cake pop sticks

Toothpicks

2 drops food coloring (the color of your choice)

Icing stars

DIRECTIONS

1. Prepare the cake according to package instructions, mixing in the additional $\frac{1}{4}$ cup vegetable oil to the batter before pouring into the pan. Bake according to package directions.

2. Once the cake is cool to the touch, transfer to a large mixing bowl and break into crumbs. Allow it to cool completely.

3. In a medium bowl, combine the butter, sugar, vanilla, and milk. Use an electric mixer or stand mixer and beat on medium speed for about 4 minutes, until frosting is light and fluffy.

4. Add 1 cup of the frosting to the cake crumbs and beat until mixture holds

together well (save the remaining $^1/_4$ cup for decorations). Refrigerate the cake mixture for at least an hour.

5. Using your hands, shape the cake pop mixture into 36 conical shapes.

6. Melt the green candy melts according to package instructions. Dip one end of each of the cake pop sticks into the melted chocolate, then insert that end into the bottom of a cake pop. Chill in the refrigerator for 10 minutes. Dip each cake pop into the melted chocolate (you may have to remelt), making sure to cover completely.

7. Use a toothpick to create the textured look of the tree before standing upright to dry. Add a few drops of the food coloring to the left-over icing and mix well. Using a piping bag (or a plastic sandwich bag with one small corner cut off) add dots or garlands to decorate the trees.

Rockin' Christmas Music Trivia

Think you know your Christmas songs? Let's see!

1 Who sings the famous Christmas song "All I Want for Christmas Is You"?

2 In "Jingle Bell Rock," where were the jingle bells described as "dancin' and prancin'"?

3 What Christmas song includes the lyrics, "In the meadow we can build a snowman"?

4 Which band originally sang "Last Christmas"?

5 "All is calm, all is bright" is part of the opening lines to which famous Christmas carol?

6 Who had a hit with "Rockin' Around the Christmas Tree" in 1958? (*Psst*, you should know this one!)

7 What is the subtitle of "The Christmas Song" by Nat King Cole?

8 In "The Twelve Days of Christmas," what gift is given on the fifth day?

9 Who wrote the song "White Christmas"?

10 What Christmas song was originally written for Thanksgiving?

11 In the song "Frosty the Snowman," what are Frosty's eyes made of?

12 What holiday song contains the lyrics "Everyone dancing merrily in the new old-fashioned way"?

13 What song begins with the lyrics "You better watch out, you better not cry"?

14 Which Christmas song is recognized by the opening line "City sidewalks, busy sidewalks"?

15 In the song "Rudolph the Red-Nosed Reindeer," what did the other reindeer not let Rudolph do?

16 Who cowrote "Happy Xmas (War Is Over)" with John Lennon?

17 In the song "Let It Snow! Let It Snow! Let It Snow!" what is the weather like outside?

18 Which illustrious '90s boy band recorded the song "Merry Christmas, Happy Holidays"?

19 Which singer made "Feliz Navidad" a well-known Christmas song?

20 What Christmas song features the line "Faithful friends who are dear to us gather near to us once more"?

1. Mariah Carey, 2. Jingle Bell Square (also acceptable: in the frosty air), 3. "Walking in a Winter Wonderland," 4. WHAM!, 5. "Silent Night," 6. Brenda Lee, of course!, 7. "Merry Christmas to You" (also acceptable: "Chestnuts Roasting on an Open Fire"), 8. "Five golden rings," 9. Irving Berlin, 10. "Over the River and Through the Woods," 11. Coal, 12. "Rockin' Around the Christmas Tree," 13. "Santa Claus Is Comin' to Town," 14. "Silver Bells," 15. Join in any reindeer games, 16. Yoko Ono, 17. Frightful, 18. *NSYNC, 19. José Feliciano, 20. "Have Yourself a Merry Little Christmas"

"Rockin'" Covers

Since the song was released in 1958, the world has fallen in love with this catchy Christmas classic. Music artists from lots of genres have given the tune their own signature flair. See if one of your favorite artists has covered the song (because they probably have!).

DOLLY PARTON

LEANN RIMES

MILEY CYRUS

CYNDI LAUPER

JUSTIN BIEBER

KIM WILDE AND MEL SMITH

HANSON

JESSICA SIMPSON

ALY & AJ

SHE & HIM

KELLY CLARKSON

PENTATONIX

MARY J. BLIGE

MICHAEL BUBLÉ

ALABAMA

CHICAGO

MEGHAN TRAINOR

THE MAN BEHIND THE SONG:
Johnny Marks

Generations have loved the stop-motion special *Rudolph the Red-Nosed Reindeer* since it premiered on television in 1964. Viewers sway to Sam the Snowman, voiced by Burl Ives, as he sings about "Silver and Gold." They get a tear in their eyes as young reindeer Clarice tries to cheer up a blue Rudolph, reminding him "There's Always Tomorrow." And of course, who can forget the song that inspired the whole special, "Rudolph the Red-Nosed Reindeer"? These classic Christmas songs were written by the same songwriter behind "A Holly Jolly Christmas" and "Rockin' Around the Christmas Tree"—Johnny Marks. If there were a Christmas Hall of Fame, Johnny's portrait would certainly be in it!

Deck the halls with boughs of holly

Home Decor &
GREENERY

Adorning Your Home Inside and Out

With glossy green leaves and ruby red berries, holly fits the Christmas decoration brief perfectly.

The plant has been admired for centuries, long before folks incorporated it into Christmas decorations. Ancient Druids admired the way holly kept its foliage and berries even in the harshest winter weather. They believed hanging the plant in their homes would bring good luck, although they avoided cutting down the entire holly tree, as this might bring bad luck. Eventually holly was brought into early Christian tradition as a symbol of Christ's sacrifice for humankind. In the centuries since, holly has been a central decoration in the celebration of the holiday.

Holly has a long lifespan, making it a fresh yet low-maintenance part of any home's Christmas decor. If you live in North America, Europe, or Asia, there may be wild holly growing just a short walk away, ready to adorn the halls and walls of your home.

Fun Fact!

The American holly was named the official state tree of Delaware in 1939. In the 1930s, Delaware was the holly capital of the US and was home to more than 8,500 wreathmakers working in the business.

Fun Fact!

The music for "Deck the Halls" comes from a traditional Welsh melody from the sixteenth century, but the lyrics were written in 1862 by a Scottish musician named Thomas Oliphant.

Fun Fact!

While toxic to humans, dogs, and cats, holly berries are a vital source of food for birds like thrushes and blackbirds. Holly berries ripen in winter and usually contain four seeds each. When birds eat the berries, they scatter the seeds and help new holly trees grow.

Fun Fact!

The phrase "deck the halls" comes from the early church's term for Christmas Eve, *templa exornatur*, meaning "churches are decked."

Fun Fact!

Cranberries have been consumed at Thanksgiving dinners since the time of the first pilgrims. Native to North America, they are harvested between September and December, making them perfect for the holidays. Their bright red berries provide a merry color amid the gray of winter, and their sweetness offers a nice complement to traditional Christmas turkey.

Baked Brie with Cranberries

PREP TIME: 5 MINUTES / TOTAL TIME: 30 MINUTES / SERVES: 4 TO 8

Creamy Brie meets the tangy sweetness of cranberries in this cheery, crowd-pleasing appetizer. Best served warm and melty, straight from the oven, with a platter of crackers and fresh fruit.

1/2 cup granulated sugar

1/4 cup balsamic vinegar

2 cups fresh cranberries, rinsed

1 13.2-ounce wheel of Brie cheese

▶ DIRECTIONS

1. Preheat oven to 400 degrees F. Adjust the oven racks to the upper and the middle positions. Line a sheet pan with parchment paper.

2. In a medium mixing bowl, combine the sugar and balsamic vinegar. Add the cranberries and toss until well-coated. Pour them onto a sheet pan in a single layer and place on the upper rack of the oven to roast for 25 minutes, stirring halfway through cooking.

3. Place the Brie wheel in a round baking dish (or pie pan) and bake at the same time as the cranberries, on the middle rack of the oven.

4. Remove the cranberries and the Brie from the oven. Immediately top the Brie wheel with the roasted cranberry and balsamic mixture. Serve with pita crackers or toasted baguette slices.

Add Some Jolly Around Your Home

Holly doesn't just have to deck the halls and walls. Place a sprig or two anywhere you need a festive touch.

- Add holly inside a centerpiece.
- Fill your flower arrangement with pops of red.
- Spruce up a cookie tray.
- Add a simple adornment to napkins or gifts.

CREATE AN EYE-CATCHING MANTEL FOR ALL WINTER LONG

A mantel often serves as the visual centerpiece of a room, especially during the cold winter months when folks tend to gather around the fire. Adding decor to your mantel sets the tone for the entire room, evoking warmth and comfort as you express your personal aesthetic.

It's easy to update the look all winter long too. Don't want to keep Christmas vibes going? No problem! Transition out the reds and golds but opt to keep the greens and browns for a seasonally appropriate theme. Keep the soft lights and textures to maintain comfy, cozy feels all winter long.

ADD THESE ELEMENTS TO CREATE A MAGICAL MANTEL:

- **Pops of nature.** Garlands of evergreens, holly berries, pinecones, and bare branches showcase the beauty and serenity of the season.
- **Soft lighting.** Use small lights here, like votive candles and fairy lights. These create a warm glow when daylight fades.
- **Elements that express your personal style.** Meaningful ornaments and tchotchkes, Christmas stockings, holiday cards, bunting, word art—these touches make your mantel uniquely yours.
- **A centerpiece above the mantel.** A wreath, a large piece of art, a mirror—add a pop of wow to your mantel with a centerpiece that brings the look together.

Merry Berry Pavlova for Christmas

PREP TIME: 30 MINUTES / TOTAL TIME: 2 1/2 HOURS / SERVES: 8 TO 10

This layered dessert might look fancy and complicated, but it's pretty easy to make—not to mention forgiving in the decorating department. Layer luscious cream and tart berries with light and crisp meringues for a showstopping dessert with a festival of flavor and texture.

4 large egg whites, room temperature

1/2 teaspoon cream of tartar

1 1/4 cups sugar, divided

1 tablespoon cornstarch

1 teaspoon lemon juice

1 1/4 cups heavy whipping cream

3 cups fresh berries

DIRECTIONS

1. Preheat oven to 300 degrees F. Line a cookie sheet with parchment paper.

2. Place the egg whites in a large bowl. Add the cream of tartar and beat on medium speed until soft peaks form. Gradually add in 1 cup of the sugar and continue beating until stiff, glossy peaks form. Fold in the cornstarch and lemon juice.

3. Divide the meringue evenly into two portions and use a spatula to spread each into a circle about 1 1/2 to 2 inches thick on the prepared cookie sheet. Bake until the meringue is set and dry, 30 to 45 minutes. Turn off the oven and leave the meringue inside. Do not open the oven door for 1 hour.

4. Remove from the oven and let the meringue cool completely.

5. Once the meringue is cool, pour the cream into a large mixing bowl. Beat

Fun Fact! Pavlovas were invented in Australia, which is why they often use "summer" berries for Christmas recipes!

the cream until it begins to thicken. Add the remaining 1/4 cup of sugar and beat until soft peaks form.

6. Transfer one meringue circle to a serving plate. Layer half of the whipped cream over the meringue and top with half of the fresh berries. Place the second meringue circle on top and add the remaining whipped cream and berries. Refrigerate until ready to serve.

Rockin' around
the Christmas tree

Happy
CHRISTMAS
Morning!

Unwrap the Magic of Christmas

No matter if you're age four, thirty-four, or eighty-four, waking up on Christmas morning just hits different. There's so much to look forward to—no work, time together, savoring a slow Christmas breakfast, and sipping cups of hot cocoa or holiday mimosa. The thrill of opening presents when you're small somehow grows even greater when you become an adult and watch your own little ones tear open their packages and rifle through their stockings and marvel in wonder. The only way it could grow more magical is to look outside and see the world blanketed in white.

Of all the Christmas traditions, one of the most beloved is hanging stockings by the fire and finding them filled with goodies on Christmas morning. But how did this tradition come to be? According to legend, a father of three girls had recently lost his wife and was having a hard time making ends meet. St. Nicholas was wandering through the town and heard what had happened to this family. He knew the father would refuse any charity directly, so one night, St. Nicholas slid down the family's chimney and saw the girls' freshly laundered stockings drying by the fire. He left coins in the stockings and climbed back up the chimney, unnoticed. The next

morning, the girls woke up and discovered these unexpected gifts and showed their father, who was overcome by this mysterious generosity.

Where did this story come from? How true is it? No one knows. But one thing's for certain: The generosity of St. Nicholas lives on today. And you can see his miracle of giving every single Christmas morning.

Sausage and Egg Breakfast Casserole

PREP TIME: 45 MINUTES / TOTAL TIME: 3 1/2 HOURS / SERVES: 10

A perfect make-ahead meal for Christmas morning. Assemble the casserole the night before, pop it into the oven while you're opening gifts, and you'll have a piping-hot breakfast when you're ready to eat.

1 loaf Italian bread

1 pound pork breakfast sausage

1 small onion, peeled and diced

12 large eggs

4 cups milk

1½ teaspoons salt

1 teaspoon freshly ground black pepper

½ tablespoon hot sauce

3 cups extra sharp cheddar cheese, divided

▶ DIRECTIONS

1. Preheat the oven to 450 degrees F and move the rack to the middle position. Grease a 9 x 13-inch baking dish.

2. Tear or cut the bread loaf into bite-size pieces and spread them in a single layer over two cookie sheets. Bake for 8 to 10 minutes or until golden brown, tossing the bread and rotating the sheets about halfway through baking. Remove from the oven and allow to cool.

3. Meanwhile, in a large skillet over medium heat, brown the sausage, stirring occasionally, until no longer pink in the middle, 5 to 10 minutes. Add the onion and cook 5 minutes longer, until translucent.

4. In a large mixing bowl, whisk the eggs. Add the milk, salt, pepper, and hot sauce and whisk well.

Pro Tip: This recipe will require two 9 x 13-inch baking dishes and can be prepared up to 24 hours in advance.

5. To the prepared baking dish, add half of the toasted bread. Top the bread with half of the sausage mixture and 1 cup of the cheese. Add the remaining bread, the remaining sausage mixture, then the remaining cheese. Pour the egg and milk mixture evenly over the casserole. Wrap the casserole with plastic wrap and place another 9 x 13-inch baking dish on top, and place the dishes on a rimmed cookie sheet. Add canned goods or something heavy to the top dish to weigh it down.

6. Refrigerate for at least one hour or up to 24 hours.

7. When ready to bake, remove the casserole from the refrigerator while preheating the oven to 350 degrees F.

8. Remove the canned goods and plastic wrap and bake for 1 hour to 1 hour and 15 minutes, until top is golden brown. Allow it to cool for at least 15 minutes before serving.

Create Your Own Stockings

TOTAL TIME: 2 HOURS / MAKES: 2 STOCKINGS

Create instant heirlooms that you'll cherish for years to come. A perfect activity for kids to join.

Craft paper

Pencil

Felt-tipped marker

Scissors

2 to 3 yards natural cotton muslin or burlap craft fabric

All-purpose sewing thread

1 needle for hand-stitching

4 feet cotton ribbon

Iron

1/2 yard polyester batting fabric

1 or 2 felt fabric craft sheets

▶ INSTRUCTIONS

1. Using craft paper, sketch 2 stocking patterns, various sizes or both the same, or print out available patterns online. Cut out the patterns.

2. Lay out fabric, folded in half and flattened down, with right sides of fabric together. Place pattern pieces down and pin or hold in place as you trace around them with a pencil. Cut the fabric pieces to shape.

3. Using a 1/4-inch running stitch, sew fabric pieces together around the sides and bottom of each stocking, leaving the top open by 2 inches.

4. At the top of each stocking, fold down the outside raw edges of fabric twice and flatten. Pin down or use a hot iron to keep fabric in place.

5. At the top sides of each stocking, sew on the ends of the ribbon, right sides

Pro Tip: This DIY craft is flexible for any level of experience. It is meant to be rustic, fun, creative, and perfectly imperfect!

facing together, to form a handle from one side of the stocking. Turn stockings right side out.

6. Sew raw hems to the insides of the stockings using a rough cross-stitch.

7. Add embellishments including strips of batting or additional ribbon if desired, using a slip stitch. Sew on decorative felt shapes as desired.

Festive Fancy Mimosas

PREP TIME: 15 MINUTES / TOTAL TIME: 8 1/2 HOURS/ SERVES: 4

A holiday twist on a brunch favorite. These mimosas rely on simple but beautiful ice cubes that you make ahead. Then let your guests pour their own sparkling wine when they wish. A merry morning, indeed!

1 cup orange juice

1 bottle sparkling wine, divided

4 orange slices

1/4 cup red currants or fresh cranberries

1 large sprig rosemary, cut into 4 pieces

▶ DIRECTIONS

1. Add the orange juice and 1/2 cup sparkling wine to a pitcher and stir; set aside.
2. In each of 4 cavities of a large circle or square ice cube mold, add an orange slice, 1/4 of the red currants or cranberries, and top with a piece of rosemary.
3. Pour the orange juice and sparkling wine mixture over the fruit and rosemary and freeze for at least 8 hours.
4. Remove the ice cubes from the mold and place in coupe or margarita glasses. Fill the glasses with the remaining sparkling wine.

When Christmas Isn't Like It Usually Is

Sometimes the holiday you have isn't the holiday you anticipated. Maybe you're spending Christmas in a new-to-you home after an unexpected move. Maybe the holiday takes you somewhere exciting, like a ski cabin or the beach, and you're not sure how to celebrate this year. Or perhaps you're spending Christmas morning next to the hospital bed of a loved one.

No matter why your holiday is different this year, experiencing Christmas in a new way can leave you with complicated feelings. But there are still ways to make the holiday meaningful and joyful. Here are some things you could try:

- Acknowledge your feelings
- Adjust your expectations
- Create a cozy environment
- Embrace new traditions
- Stay connected to loved ones
- Help someone else
- Plan for the future
- Take care of yourself

A Christmas in a new place or circumstance can be challenging. But when you roll with the situation in front of you and find new ways to celebrate, you can still find joy and meaning in the season.

Have a happy holiday

Cozy CHRISTMAS GATHERINGS

Enjoy Celebrations with Laughter and Love

You don't need permission for this, but here it is anyway:

You have permission to *not* throw a Christmas party that's extra.

It's true. *Extra* is not necessary!

You don't have to throw a party that's all about gifts.

You don't have to throw a party that costs a trillion dollars.

You don't have to throw a party and invite every single person in your phone contacts.

There are so many ways to celebrate the Christmas season. Someone in your circle is going to throw that over-the-top party. And good for them! Those parties are fun. But if you're in a season where gathering a small group for pasta and good conversation sounds more your speed, then absolutely, do that. If you'd rather center your activity on *making* something instead of *consuming* something, go for it! Heck, you can even stay in, put on your soft clothes, and settle on the couch for a mindless Christmas movie with your dog by your side. There's

room for every kind of gathering on the holiday season calendar, even if it's a party of one. The only requirement is to enjoy the season, however that looks for you this year.

Remember, sometimes the happiest Christmases are the coziest. Because after all, there's so much wonder to be found in the small moments.

Potato, Leek, and Bacon Soup

PREP TIME: 20 MINUTES / TOTAL TIME: 1 HOUR / SERVES: 8

Nothing says cozy Christmas gathering like a warm, savory soup on the stove. Flavorful bacon, sautéed leeks, and a creamy broth will be just what you want on a cold winter day.

8 russet potatoes, peeled and cubed

8 cups chicken broth

1/2 pound thick-cut bacon, chopped

3 leeks, sliced, tops of stems discarded

1/2 cup heavy cream

1/2 cup sour cream

1/2 teaspoon kosher salt or to taste

1/2 teaspoon freshly ground black pepper or to taste

1 tablespoon fresh parsley, roughly chopped

▶ DIRECTIONS

1. Place the potatoes and chicken broth in a large stockpot over medium-hig heat. Boil for 20 to 25 minutes or until potatoes are fork tender.

2. Meanwhile, fry the bacon in a skillet over medium-high heat until crispy, about 5 minutes, stirring frequently. Transfer the bacon to paper towels to drain. Do not clean out the skillet.

3. Add the leeks to the skillet used for the bacon and sauté for 5 to 8 minutes or until translucent. Remove from heat and set aside.

4. When the potatoes are tender, stir in the bacon, leeks, heavy cream, and sour cream. Season the soup with salt and pepper. Cook for another 5 minutes until heated through. Garnish with fresh parsley.

HOST A CHRISTMAS CRAFT DAY

finger foods, and provide a h chocolate or cider drink bar s guests can help themselves. Har

EASY

- Ornament decorating
- Homemade Christmas cards
- DIY gift bags and tags
- Assembling homemade food gifts: hot chocolate mix, cookie mix, flavored popcorn, etc.
- Holiday garland and bunting
- Christmas jar "snow globe"

EXPERT

- Christmas jewelry, like earrings and necklaces
- Candle making
- Wreath or centerpiece making
- Next-level gift wrapping
- Embroidered Christmas cards
- Intricate paper stars

Merry and Bright Idea

Decide who's going to provide materials for the crafts—you, or your guests. Consider designating a "station captain" who's responsible for bringing the materials for their station.

Jingle Bingo for the Win

Spice up your Christmas movie marathon with bingo. When it's frigid outside, there's something extra cozy about snuggling into a soft chair with a delicious snack to watch a slate of Christmas movies. Adding bingo into the mix adds an extra layer of enjoyment.

1. CHOOSE YOUR MOVIE.

You could go for a Christmas classic that everyone's seen like *How the Grinch Stole Christmas* or *It's a Wonderful Life*—or you could choose the latest Hallmark Christmas movie so that everyone has to stay on their game the whole time (no relying on memory here).

2. CREATE (OR FIND) YOUR BINGO CARDS.

You can get as intricate as you want, but begin by creating cards with a 5 x 5 square grid. Each square should contain a specific event, quote, character, or scene that typically occurs in Christmas movies, such as:

- A character drinks hot cocoa
- Someone says, "Merry Christmas"

- A snowball fight happens
- A character dresses as Santa Claus
- Someone decorates a Christmas tree
- Someone shows up in an ugly Christmas sweater
- A couple kisses under the mistletoe
- A misunderstanding or mix-up occurs (gasp!)
- Someone mentions the North Pole
- A miracle happens

Remember to put a free space in the center and create different variations of the cards so that everyone's grid looks different. What's the fun if everyone hits bingo at the same time?

3. PRINT OUT OR SEND A LINK TO EACH PARTICIPANT.

A small step, but a necessary one. If you're going with paper sheets, set out some pencils, pens, stickers, or highlighters so that guests can mark their papers as they go.

4. DON'T FORGET THE PRIZES!

To up the stakes, give the winner a stocking filled with Christmas candy, an ornament, or a gift card.

Everyone dancin'
merrily

Holiday

DANCE PARTY

Jingle All the Way to the Dance Floor

No matter where you are on the globe, you'll see it: When humans are happy, we dance. And Christmastime has been a season of dancing for quite a long time. From the lively Christmas balls that Jane Austen attended in Regency-era England to art pieces like *The Nutcracker* ballet, dancing and Christmas go hand in hand.

Cultures around the world celebrate the Christmas season with their own folk dances. In Denmark, it's customary to dance around the tree on Christmas Eve, singing traditional Danish songs. People in the Caribbean celebrate Jonkonnu, a festival between Christmas and New Year's filled with bright masks and costumes as they dance to music with lots of percussion. In Scotland, many perform traditional dances to Gaelic music sometimes with partners but mostly in groups—sometimes even beside a blazing bonfire.

No wonder we need so much great music to accompany us through the season—we've got some dancing to do! And you don't need a formal dance floor or a catering company to throw a great dance party, just a clear space and a great playlist. So gather your people, turn up the music, and dance the night away.

HOST A FANCY CHRISTMAS PARTY THIS YEAR

New Year's gets all the love for over-the-top parties with a touch of elegance. But let's face it: Sometimes during the Christmas season you're ready to ditch the ugly sweater and go for a little more glam. Here are some ideas to class up your Christmas party.

- **SEND INVITATIONS:** Send out beautifully designed invitations that match your theme at least a few weeks before the party. Holiday calendars fill up fast, so do this early. A digital invite is easy for tracking RSVPs, but a printed invitation will give a more bespoke feel.
- **CHOOSE THE ATTIRE:** Ask your guests to dress for a cocktail party. Choose a theme for the party, like Winter Wonderland, Vintage Christmas, or Black-Tie Bash.
- **DECORATE WITH ELEGANCE:** Pay attention to color scheme (silver and blue, gold and silver, or the classic red and green). Use candles or fairy lights to create a warm atmosphere. Create a tablescape with the fanciest wares, cloth napkins, tapers, and name cards.
- **CURATE A SOPHISTICATED MENU:** Break out your most refined dishes. Remember to be inclusive to food allergies and dietary restrictions; encourage guests to list any needs on their RSVP.
- **PLAN ENTERTAINMENT:** Put on a festive playlist or hire live musicians to elevate the ambiance. Consider hosting a silent auction to benefit a worthy organization. Include a photo for memory-making.
- **GIVE OUT PARTY FAVORS:** As the party wraps up, hand each guest a small, elegant gift like chocolates, an ornament, or a bottle of wine.

Yuletide Groove Games

Get your guests to jingle-bell rock out with these holiday-themed games. Festive beats and a dose of holiday fun will keep dancers of all ages out of their seats and on their feet.

SANTA'S DANCE-OFF

Show off your solo moves! Ask dancers to choose a Christmas song and groove their hearts out for thirty seconds. A panel of judges can decide who has the most impressive moves.

ROCKIN' AROUND THE CHRISTMAS TREE FREEZE

Have dancers gather around the Christmas tree while the host turns on a playlist. Guests dance to the music—until the host hits Stop! When the music stops playing, dancers must run to touch the tree. Whoever touches the tree last is eliminated. The last player standing wins.

CHRISTMAS CAROL CHARADES

Write the names of popular Christmas songs onto slips of paper and place them in a bowl. Divide players into teams. Players blindly choose a song, then dance and act their hearts out as their team tries to guess the song title. The team with the most points wins.

HOLIDAY DANCE-A-THON

Only for the bold. Grab a partner, turn on your favorite playlist, and see which couple can dance the longest without stopping. Set a time limit for easier play—or be cutthroat and see how long your players can go.

Try This: If you cannot find pear juice, try apple juice or apple juice cocktail.

Rockin' Christmas Punch

TOTAL TIME: 10 MINUTES / SERVES: 4

Liven up the drink station with this bright and festive drink. Tart cranberries pair with natural sweetness from the oranges and pears for a light and elegant punch.

$1\frac{1}{2}$ cups pear juice

$\frac{3}{4}$ cup tequila

$\frac{1}{2}$ cup club soda

$\frac{1}{4}$ cup lemon juice

1 tablespoon simple syrup

$\frac{1}{4}$ teaspoon vanilla extract

$\frac{1}{4}$ teaspoon ground cinnamon

$\frac{1}{2}$ pear, sliced thin horizontally

$\frac{1}{2}$ orange, sliced thin horizontally

$\frac{1}{2}$ cup fresh cranberries, frozen

▶ DIRECTIONS

Combine the pear juice, tequila, club soda, lemon juice, simple syrup, vanilla, and cinnamon in a pitcher and gently stir. Add in the sliced fruit. Divide the frozen cranberries into 4 glasses. Pour punch into glasses.

Merry and Bright Idea

Dial up or down the fancy with the glasses you use for serving. Use a coupe or champagne flute to dial it up, or a stemless wine glass, a lowball, or even a mug to create a more intimate night.

Crostini with Sautéed Mushrooms and Fresh Goat Cheese

PREP TIME: 10 MINUTES / TOTAL TIME: 30 MINUTES / MAKES: 20

In this appetizer, creamy goat cheese and garlic mushrooms are slathered onto toasted bread slices for a delectably crunchy bite.

1 baguette, cut into 20 diagonal slices

3 tablespoons extra virgin olive oil, divided

1 tablespoon butter

2 medium shallots, sliced

1 pound button mushrooms, sliced

2 cloves garlic, minced

2 tablespoons lemon juice

2 teaspoons fresh thyme leaves, plus additional for garnish

Kosher salt to taste

Ground black pepper to taste

4 ounces goat cheese

1/4 cup pine nuts (or walnut pieces), toasted

DIRECTIONS

1. Preheat oven to 425 degrees F.

2. Brush both sides of the baguette slices with 2 tablespoons of the olive oil. Place the slices on a large sheet in a single layer and bake for 5 to 10 minute

3. Meanwhile, heat the butter and remaining olive oil in a large skillet over medium-high heat. Add shallots and cook just until translucent, stirring frequently, about 2 minutes. Add the mushrooms and continue cooking, stirring frequently, until browned and tender, about 10 minutes.

4. Stir in the garlic, lemon juice, and fresh thyme. Season with salt and pepper and continue to cook another minute. Remove from heat.

5. Spread each crostini with the goat cheese, then top with the mushrooms.
6. Sprinkle thyme leaves on top and garnish with pine nuts (or walnuts).

CREATE A DIY BACKDROP FOR SOCIAL MEDIA–WORTHY PHOTO OPS

Want a fun and festive way to capture shareable holiday memories? Create a DIY photo booth.

YOU'LL NEED:

- **BACKDROP FABRIC OR PAPER:** Use a large piece of fabric (a white sheet, a swath of red velvet, or green cloth). You could also use wrapping paper in a Christmas pattern.
- **CHRISTMAS DECOR**: Gather decorations like tinsel, holly, garlands, fairy lights, ornaments, and Christmas wreaths.
- **REUSABLE ADHESIVE HOOKS OR TAPE:** So you can hang the backdrop and decorations.
- **PROPS**: Think Santa hats, reindeer antlers, fake snow, and holiday-themed signs to add some fun to the photos.
- **CAMERA STAND OR TRIPOD:** To keep your camera or phone steady and at the right height for photos.
- **RING LIGHT**: So your guests will show up in their photos.

CHOOSE YOUR SETUP LOCATION

Find a wall with enough space for the backdrop. Add a ring light if needed to ensure good lighting.

HANG THE BACKDROP

Use reusable adhesive hooks or strong tape to fix the fabric or wrapping paper to the wall. Make sure your backdrop is wrinkle-free and covers a wide area so that guests fit in the photos.

CREATE A FESTIVE FRAME

Use larger decorations like garlands or string lights to create a frame around the backdrop.

ADD DECORATIONS

Hang ornaments, stars, or small wreaths directly on the backdrop. Consider placing small Christmas trees or wrapped gifts on the floor in front of the backdrop.

SET UP THE CAMERA

Put your camera or phone on a tripod and make sure it's aligned with the center of the backdrop. Designate a photographer or set up a remote shutter so guests can photograph themselves easily.

PREP THE PROPS

Set props near the booth so guests can grab them before stepping in front of the camera.

TEST THE SETUP

Take a few test shots to make sure your setup looks great. Adjust the lighting, decorations, or camera angle as needed.

Merry and Bright Idea

Help guests take home their memories instantly. Place an instant camera near the booth or set up a small station where guests can print their digital photos.

In the new old-fashioned way

Mixing CHRISTMAS Past & Present

Cherish the Classics; Make New Memories

"The new old-fashioned way"—that's the feeling every Christmas evokes, or at least the kind of Christmas we hope for. We find the Christmas season so special because it takes us back to the past, just for a little while. We remember decorating a gingerbread house with our cousins. We remember how strong our dads looked schlepping in a pile of wood for the fire. We remember our mothers making sure that every person at the Christmas table had enough to eat, then taking a plate to an elderly neighbor who was under the weather. We remember the warmth and love and values that held us through our most tender years.

But as we get a few more Christmases under our belts, here's the fun little secret we learn: Every Christmas is an opportunity to make new memories, to begin new traditions, and to find hope and joy that sometimes fade in harder seasons. We get to make the holidays our own, whether that's by hosting an all-dessert Christmas gathering, making gingerbread house cookies instead of constructing and decorating a 3D house, or dreaming up our own version of an Advent calendar with a blend of past and present.

So this season, celebrate Christmas your own way by marrying the cozy warm Christmases of years past with the thrill of all things new.

A CHRISTMAS WITH VINTAGE VIBES

Create an atmosphere brimming with cozy nostalgia that brings the magic of yesteryear to your celebration. Here's how:

- **ORNAMENTS AND DECOR:** Go shopping in a vintage store on the hunt for ornaments from years past. Look for items like ceramic baubles, frosted glass ornaments, baubles with glittery/interesting patterns, and wooden Christmas ornaments. You might even find vintage glassware or dishes to set your table with. Shop carefully to avoid lead or uranium glass.
- **LIGHTS:** Colored Christmas lights with oversized bulbs are a must. If you can't find an old string of lights (that doesn't have a bulb or two burned out), the Tru-Tone Bulbs company makes a beautiful throwback alternative that is LED and much more energy efficient.
- **COLOR SCHEMES:** Lean into those cheery reds and deep greens of yesteryear to evoke the charm of Christmases past. Or break out of the traditional and embrace tones that nod to mid-century vibes, like pastels, teals, pinks, and goldenrods.

- **FOOD:** Eggnog, sugar cookies, gingerbread. If you're brave, make a fruitcake.

- **WRAPPING PAPER:** Use colors and prints that evoke an old-fashioned feel. You can even use wrapping paper from your favorite movie characters, like Peanuts or the Grinch, to instantly call back the classics.
- **TUNES:** The original Christmas songs from the 1940s to the 1960s can instantly transport you to the holidays of your childhood. Dial up Nat King Cole, Bing Crosby, Frank Sinatra, and Gene Autry.

Apple Cider Old-Fashioned

TOTAL TIME: 5 MINUTES / SERVES: 1

Crisp apple flavor and warm spices add a touch of holiday sweetness to this Christmas cocktail. A new old-fashioned favorite!

2 ounces whiskey

2 ounces apple cider

2 dashes bitters

2 thin apple wedges

1 orange slice

1 cinnamon stick

DIRECTIONS

In a lowball glass, combine the whiskey, apple cider, and bitters. Add ice and gently stir. Add in the apples, orange, and cinnamon stick to serve.

Fun Fact!

The old-fashioned cocktail originated in the early 1800s. When cocktails started getting more complex in the 1860s, drinkers began asking for the simpler drink of the past, thus providing its nostalgic name.

Gingerbread House Cookies

PREP TIME: 45 MINUTES / TOTAL TIME: 3 HOURS / MAKES: 12 COOKIES

You don't have to make a whole gingerbread house if you don't want to. Make gingerbread house cookies instead!

FOR THE COOKIES

1 cup butter, softened

2 tablespoons shortening

1 1/3 cups packed brown sugar

2 tablespoons granulated sugar

1 large egg

1 egg yolk (save white for icing)

1/4 cup molasses

1 teaspoon vanilla extract

1 teaspoon ground cinnamon

1 1/8 teaspoon ground ginger

1/8 teaspoon ground cloves

1 teaspoon cornstarch

1/4 teaspoon baking soda

1/2 teaspoon salt

3 cups all-purpose flour, plus 1 1/2 tablespoons

FOR THE ICING

1 large egg white

1 teaspoon lime juice

1 teaspoon almond extract

3 cups powdered sugar

▶ DIRECTIONS

1. Cream the butter, shortening, both sugars, egg, egg yolk, molasses, and vanilla with an electric mixer on medium-low speed until well combined and smooth. Add in the spices, cornstarch, baking soda, salt, and flour to the wet ingredients and continue to mix until a stiff dough forms. Shape into a ball, cover with plastic wrap, and refrigerate for at least 2 hours.

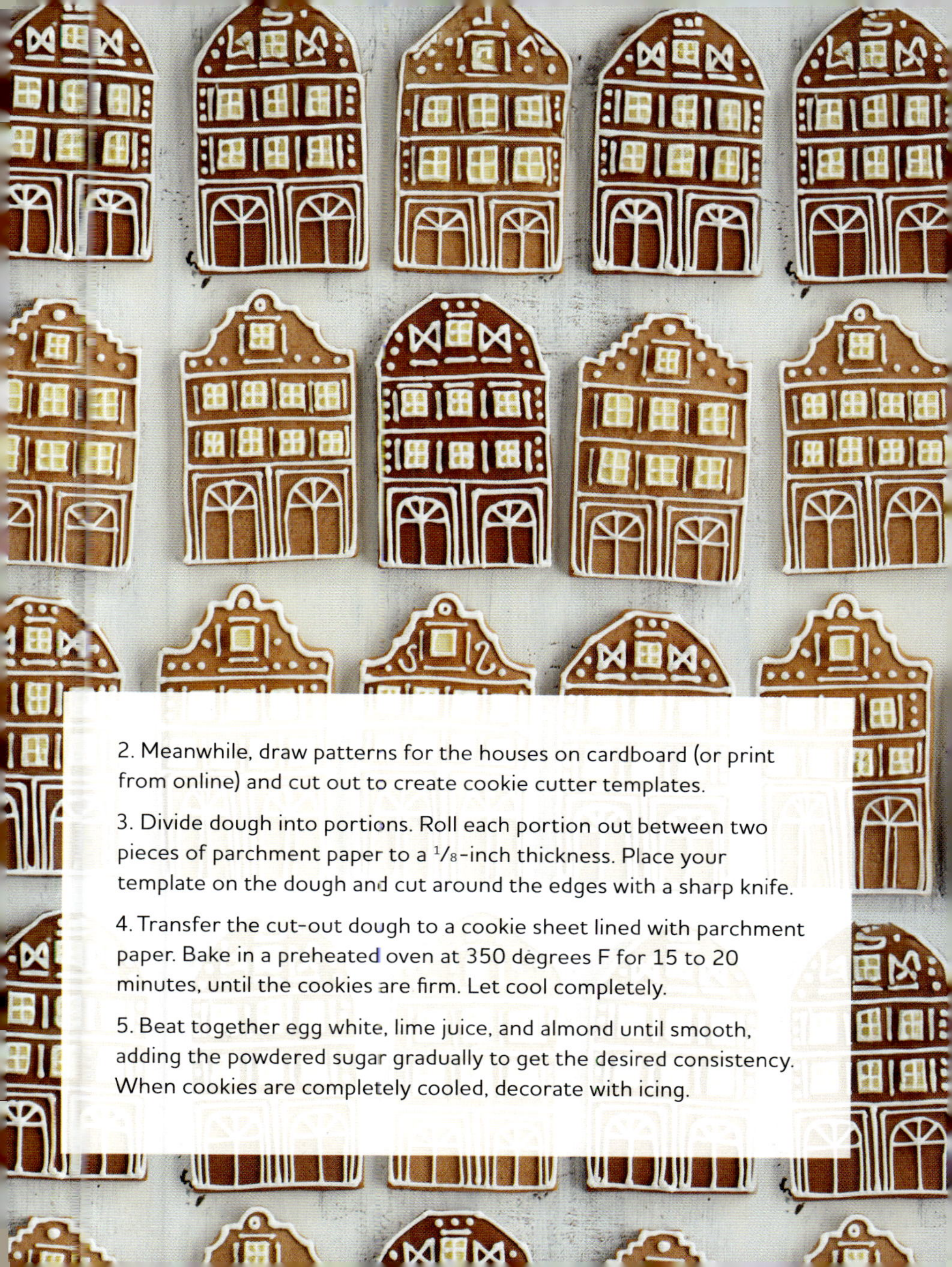

2. Meanwhile, draw patterns for the houses on cardboard (or print from online) and cut out to create cookie cutter templates.

3. Divide dough into portions. Roll each portion out between two pieces of parchment paper to a $\frac{1}{8}$-inch thickness. Place your template on the dough and cut around the edges with a sharp knife.

4. Transfer the cut-out dough to a cookie sheet lined with parchment paper. Bake in a preheated oven at 350 degrees F for 15 to 20 minutes, until the cookies are firm. Let cool completely.

5. Beat together egg white, lime juice, and almond until smooth, adding the powdered sugar gradually to get the desired consistency. When cookies are completely cooled, decorate with icing.

Merry and Bright Idea

Not sure what to put in your Advent calendar? Go for a theme! Tuck in holiday chocolates for the candy lover, tea bags for the drink maven, lip balm and gloss for the makeup girlies, and Matchbox cars for those with a need for speed.

DIY Advent Calendar

TOTAL TIME: 1 TO 2 HOURS / MAKES: 1 CALENDAR

Who said Advent calendars had to cost much? This DIY version lets you customize the gifts your people open each day, with a price tag that's a lot easier on your wallet.

- Crepe paper streamer
- Masking tape
- 25 flat Kraft paper bags; approximately 4 x 6 inches
- Felt-tipped marker, white
- Metallic star stickers
- School glue
- Ribbon
- Evergreen tips
- Decorative round stickers, numbered from 1 to 25
- Small, lightweight Advent gifts: candy, trinkets, or toys
- 25 miniature clothespins
- Assorted ornaments for decorating

INSTRUCTIONS

1. Cut 6 strips of desired lengths of crepe paper streamer and tape horizontally to wall or door at desired heights.
2. Decorate each bag front as desired and add a trinket or gift to each bag.
3. Neatly fold down tops of bags and seal with a single numbered sticker, from 1 to 25, adding additional decoration if desired.
4. Using miniature clothespins, neatly attach prepared bags to streamer strips. Decorate with additional festive ornaments.

Join Brenda Lee's Email List!
SIGN UP TO RECEIVE UPDATES

rockin' around
rockin' around
rockin' around

rockin' around